CONSCIOUS TRANSFORMATION

12 Remarkable & Inspiring Stories of the Power to Transform Your Life

COMPILED BY:

UCHECHI EZURIKE-BOSSE

DIANNE TAYLOR | JENNIFER GASKELL | KATE LESSLIE

LINDSAY COUTURE | MAKAELA MOORE | DR. MIKE COULAS

FRANCES ADAMSON | JO MAZGAY | SARAH STERNBERG

JENN LAFORET | LIZ JAKOI | FRAN STEYN

My Empowered Living
www.myempoweredliving.com
info@myempoweredliving.com

To order additional copies of this book:
orders@myempoweredliving.com

Paperback ISBN: 978-1-9992039-4-8
Digital ISBN: 978-1-9992039-5-5

TABLE OF CONTENTS

INTRODUCTION
by Uchechi Ezurike-Bosse

It never ceases to amaze me, every year when I put out a call for my co-authoring book project, the caliber of people that show up for it. Moving and powerful stories that I know will inspire and impact lives. It is truly an honour and privilege to create this space, through the pages of this book, to share their stories with you.

The theme of Conscious Transformation was one that resonated with many people. The truth is that people, possibly you, desire to change some aspect of their life. It could be health and wellness, relationships, wealth and career, you name it. There are countless things people are looking to change.

So, what is conscious transformation?

For me, it's the act of deliberate creation. Consciously choosing the results you want and showing up for it, despite outside circumstances and influences.

It's clear that many people are struggling right now. The world is full of so much angst, polarity and toxic energy. It's hard not to allow it all to overwhelm you and fall prey to its negativity.

My hope with this book, is that it gives you the space to escape toxic energy. To inspire you to know that anything you wish to transform is attainable for you.

The stories you will read throughout the pages of this book, will show you how possible it is for you to transform any area of your life.

The incredible women and man in this book share tools, strategies and skills of how they've been able to consciously transform their lives. Their extraordinary stories of resilience, passion, courage and strength will inspire you and be evidence of what's truly achievable for you.

Please remember, dear reader. No matter what is happening in your life at this very moment. No matter your past, your programming and limiting beliefs that's holding you back. YOU, yes you have the ability to transform it. But it takes awareness and powerful tools to support you, which you will find through the pages of this book.

I know you will see yourself through the stories shared. And I truly hope these stories of conscious transformation will be your catalyst and reflect back to you what's truly available for you.

It's time to get excited about the possibility that waits you. It's time to consciously transform your life!

Uchechi Ezurike-Bosse
Author, International Speaker,
Strategist & Entrepreneur

PART 1

SELF-REALIZATION

DIANNE TAYLOR

Dianne is a compassionate, intuitive coach and mentor who works with female lawyers and other professionals to help them stop the cycle of stress and overwhelm; empowering them to take back control of their lives from the multiple demands of work and family, to finally start achieving their dream goals.

Experience from over 30 years as a lawyer and business owner, 15 years studying martial arts and Zen philosophy, and being a survivor of long term domestic violence gives Dianne a unique perspective from which she is able to draw to help her clients transform their lives.

In order to help as many women as possible, Dianne has launched the Take Back Your Life podcast where she discusses issues such as stress, mental health, personal power, setting boundaries and self-care; sharing personal stories and practical strategies.

Dianne is passionate about helping people to be their best in life, to find the confidence and strength within to face whatever is holding them back so they can achieve their full potential.

As a result she has created her unique 4-step Personal Power Process, through which she teaches her clients to find clarity on what they really want in life, what is holding them back and how to move forward to achieve their goals.

When Dianne is away from work, she can be found teaching and training in martial arts and self-defense at her local club, travelling and spending time with family and friends.

Connect with Dianne Taylor here:

www.instagram.com/dianne.g.taylor

www.diannetaylor.net

FROM THE ASHES, A PHOENIX

BY: DIANNE TAYLOR

THE CATALYST FOR CHANGE

Sometimes transformation happens gradually with small steps over time. Sometimes it can happen without you even realizing it, and other times dramatic events force you to create change.

My conscious transformation began just over four years ago now when my phone hit my head. It was thrown across the room by my then-husband and hit me mere millimetres above my right eye socket. Any lower and my eye would certainly have been damaged, maybe permanently. I have always been grateful for the blessing that it just missed my eye.

I can recall the moment of impact vividly, as if it was just yesterday. In that split-second, there was shock, clarity and decision all at once. Shock, at the violence of the act that caused injury to my face and blood to appear. Clarity, that he was never ever going to change and that the only person that could create change in my life was me. The decision, in that no matter what, my boys and I were going to be leaving that toxic space forever, that I was going to make that happen; there was no turning back.

When that phone hit my head, I felt as if I was standing in the middle of a massive sports arena, and all the lights suddenly came on at once, blinding me. I knew that if I did nothing, this would be just the first of many more incidents to come and that they would escalate in severity and frequency as things always had. If I just let it slide, I would be giving him permission to do it again and again. The words, 'the standard you walk past is the standard you accept,' instantly began ringing in my head. So in that split second, I made the conscious decision that my life would change, my sons' life would change. We were leaving, no matter what.

Thus began my conscious transformation, my decision to create change and to start again.

I made a plan, took the actions I needed to, trusted Providence for the rest to unfold in perfect timing and after 19 of the scariest days of my life, we left, never to return. So ended 36 years living with a controlling narcissist who inflicted emotional, psychological and, in the end, physical abuse on us all.

Unconscious transformation occurs all the time without us noticing the small steps over time that occur when we learn new things and change our habits and patterns. It's only when we stop and look back that we can see how the unconscious transformation unfolded and how it led us to the point where it became conscious transformation, purposeful action.

Without fully realizing it at the time, my unconscious transformation began when I turned 50. Almost one month to the day after my 50th birthday, I went back to martial arts training. I guess the seeds of this transformation were sown when I started karate training at age 39 and found something that filled me with fire and passion; that lit me up and was exactly what I was meant to be doing. When I went back at the age of 50, I thought I was totally crazy, but I was home from the minute I entered the dojo. I was in a place that was supportive, encouraging, challenging and accepting. This was where I belonged, and I made friends, a second family that I so needed; doing something that rebuilt my shattered self-confidence and belief in myself. What I hadn't realized at the time was that it would turn out to be the catalyst for ending my toxic relationship. It enabled me to withdraw from his control. In turn, his behaviour became more and more chaotic until the phone hit my head that evening.

It's truly amazing what happens when you decide to change and take a course of action. A passage that I recently added to my favourite quotes, one that keeps coming back to me, actually sums up what happened to me when I consciously decided to transform my life:

> *"The moment one definitely commits himself then Providence moves too. All sorts of things move to help one that would not normally have occurred. A whole stream of events issue from the decision, raising in one's favour all manner of unforeseen*

incidents and meetings and material assistance, which no man could have dreamed would have come his way." — W.H. Murray

Leaving a violent domestic situation is one of the most dangerous times in someone's life, but we were held and supported in the most remarkable ways. Unexpected help just appeared, and everything just simply unfolded on schedule in the most incredible ways to allow us to leave, be safe, and be saved. I am still amazed and forever grateful for everything that happened.

That was just the very eventful beginning of my transformational story.

When I made the conscious decision to leave my now ex-husband and the toxic environment we lived in, I did not fully understand that what I was doing was choosing myself. For the first time in my life, I was choosing my needs, wants and desires over his. I was choosing not to be controlled any longer. I was choosing freedom of thought, word and deed. I was choosing to value myself above all else. In the act of leaving, I was saying to myself and the world that I was worth more, that I did not have to settle for less than best, that I could have everything I ever wanted and more.

Allowing myself to believe that and to embody that decision each and every day proved to be a more challenging prospect than I thought.

So what does it take to transform?

THE JOURNEY OF A THOUSAND MILES BEGINS WITH THE FIRST STEP

There is nothing more powerful than feeling your life is moving forward, feeling that you are heading towards your goals, overcoming the obstacles in your way.

No matter the situation you are facing, the only way to gain momentum is to start by taking that first step forward.

The first step is usually the biggest and the scariest. It's more like a massive leap of faith where you cannot see where you will land. You need to trust in yourself, close your eyes and step out.

For me, in leaving my ex-husband, the biggest step was breaking the cycle of control, and until the phone hit my head, I had not been able to see the way to do it. I had been trying to change the situation from within the relationship. Once I saw the only way for change was to leave, the only person who could create change was me and that I needed to do that without delay, the next step became clear. When I took that step, a series of others opened up, and as hard as it was, I made myself take them because for us to leave, I had to.

There were only two courses of action, execute the plan to leave or stay to put up with more of the same. I found the courage within to secretly sign a lease for a house, arrange connection of services and delivery of furniture we would need. The whole time felt very surreal. I was making all of these secret plans while still running my business, keeping up with other commitments. I lived in a daze for those two-and-a-half weeks while waiting for the day our rental was ready, and we could leave.

I kept taking all the steps, no matter how scary or surreal, I kept moving forward and the relief when leaving day finally came was unbelievable.

What kept me going was the inner strength that I had re-discovered in returning to martial arts training, knowing I was up to the challenge, that I could face it and overcome it. The fact that I had overcome challenges in training had shown me again that I was capable of more, that I could go the distance no matter how big the obstacle or how scary the situation, and the last 19 days in our former home were the scariest I had ever been through. His behaviour had become more and more erratic as he struggled to regain control of the situation. I spent all of that time controlling my breathing so that I could keep the anxiety and terror at bay and get through before I had everything in place to execute my plan.

We are all masters of overthinking, trying to predict every outcome of every situation, which is just impossible and pointless. It's scary to step out, but unless you do, you will not change and grow. Believe me when I say that each step gets easier after the first one. For a while, they don't seem much easier but keep taking them, and before you know it, you will look back and wonder what you were worried about. Keep going, and you will not even recognize the person who took that first step; they will seem like someone from another life.

That's when you know you have succeeded in transforming yourself into a better, more complete version of yourself.

This is exactly what it is like for me now. I look back at that person who struggled for so long in that toxicity, who settled for less, who put up with mistreatment, who believed she was not enough, who lacked self-confidence and assertiveness, and it seems like someone else's life. Often the journey must be taken on your own, but I was fortunate to have a lifeline in my sisters who checked in each day and kept me going. Knowing they were there behind me was an amazing source of strength and helped me find courage each day, not to mention my simply incredible sons.

I now feel such love and compassion for the person I was. I just want to hug her and tell her she did such a fantastic job to stay so strong and fight as hard as she could for her sons, that she did the very best she could, and it was enough. I know what she went through to force herself to take the leaps of faith in arranging everything to leave during those final days while being terrified the whole time and trying to hold it all together in secret.

I had to forgive her so I could give her the love she deserves.

FORGIVENESS IS ABOUT YOU. IT IS A CHOICE.

What is forgiveness?

The definition of forgiveness, in part is to cease to feel resentment against an offender or to give up claim of requital.

When someone hurts us, we naturally feel hurt.

The definition of 'hurt' includes - to inflict with physical pain, to do substantial or material harm to or to cause emotional pain and anguish to.

Depending on the circumstances of how we came to be hurt, we can feel drained, weak, a sense of loss, disbelief, shock, numb, alone. We can also feel anger, injustice, rage, revenge, hate. As with any emotional event, the subconscious mind follows the pattern of what you are feeling and throws up to you all the other instances in your life when you have been hurt. This only serves to amplify your current pain.

When we are hurt, or in pain, we turn inwards; the world narrows; we retreat from the things we love and enjoy doing. The focus becomes the pain and the circumstances of the pain.

However, as in any circumstance, we have choices. We can choose to continue to live in a world bounded by pain, or we can choose to get on with the business of living.

Now, this is not to say that getting on with the business of living is an easy thing to do. It is, in fact, incredibly hard. There are considerable obstacles to overcome, changes to be made, healing to occur. It takes immense courage, but this is where personal growth occurs, where we learn about ourselves and what we are capable of, the sort of person we want to be. Experiencing circumstances and events that cause pain are part of life. How we choose to deal with them is what defines us and determines the sort of life we will lead.

The key to moving on from a place of hurt is accepting that it is a situation that you can do something about, that you can change. Yes, you are in pain, and yes, something has happened to you to cause the pain, but it is what happens next that is important. What are you going to do about it?

Staying in the place where there is pain and hurt keeps you stuck. You carry it around with you from place to place and into every new day. You keep feeling the same things, talking about the same things. You are not living; you are just on a merry-go-round, spinning around and around, ceaselessly, every day the same. You are still moving, but your life has stopped.

Accepting where you are requires you to take a fresh look at what you are doing, where you are going and deciding to change.

About six months after leaving my husband and trying to start a new life, I was still physically tied to my old life by financial matters, joint property and accounts. I realised I was getting up every day and going about things mechanically; I wasn't smiling or being happy that I was in a new place in life because all of the things that still needed to be done were on my mind. After a while, I realized I was feeling sad. Sad for the pain and damage that had been inflicted on my sons and myself, sad that so many years had been wasted. I realized I was not allowing myself to feel happy. I had finally escaped a controlled existence, and I should have been happy to be free. Instead, I was dragging around the past with me every day like a massive ball and chain. I was thinking about the things I had done wrong, what I could have done better, what more I could have, should have done for my boys, why didn't I leave sooner, on and on and on. I was stopping myself from really appreciating where I was and the potential that I now had to do whatever I wanted. I was stuck.

When that finally dawned on me, I realized I had the power to simply let it go.

For that to happen, I also realized that I had to forgive myself. I could not change anything I had done in the past. It was done, had already happened. What is past is truly past—over. The words, actions, events are finished. It is us that brings them into the future. To move forward, all I had to do was let go, step forward into each new moment free of that weight I had been hauling. So, I let go of it all and in that moment, the weight simply dropped away. I felt immediate relief and lightness of being. I forgave myself, and I did not have to revisit it. I did not have to let it destroy the beauty and potential of each new day. I was done with the past.

Forgiveness is all about you. Yes, others inflict pain and hurt on us, events cause sorrow and grief, but we cannot change the past. What we can do is determine our future.

Forgiving and moving on from events that happen to us doesn't mean that we forget what has happened. It doesn't mean that what someone else has done to us is right and can be absolved. It doesn't mean that you have to tell them you forgive them.

Forgiving is about you. It's about choosing to let go of the feelings of being hurt, choosing not to carry the pain, choosing not to colour your future with the dark colours of the past, choosing to step into the freedom and light of the next day and the next and the next.

Forgiveness allows you to love yourself, to choose to be happy and to move forward to continue to transform and live life to your highest potential.

FINDING COURAGE

Courage is the ability to do something that frightens you. It can also be defined as strength in the face of pain or grief. Other words synonymous with courage are bravery, daring, valour, audacity, boldness.

> *'Courage is resistance to fear, mastery of fear, not absence of fear'* — Mark Twain

Finding the courage to act is not always easy. Adverse situations in life can be paralysing; fear can keep us from taking action.

Even though we might be in a bad situation, we can still be afraid of taking the necessary actions to lift ourselves out of that situation. Very often, deep down, we know the action that needs to be taken, but we choose to avoid it being afraid of the consequences. The consequences might be shame, blame, ridicule, loss, anger, isolation. Yet even though the situation we are in is terrible, the consequences somehow seem worse.

In letting fear overcome the necessity to act, we give the situation or the other person power over us. They have control of our lives, our thoughts, our actions. If we are to break free of that power, we need to find courage, we need to act anyway.

This is exactly what happened to me, and fear is what kept me stuck in a violent relationship for so long. Fear of the unknown, fear of what my family would say when I told them how I had been living all those years, fear of what other people might say, how they would view me, fear of what he might do if I left. There was also fear of what would happen to my boys, fear of how it would affect them, fear of not being able to make a new life, not to mention the shame of it all. As an educated professional with her own business, how could I tell others about what my life had really been like, what had happened to us?

What I found was that courage is cumulative. Courage is built from all the different situations in life where you face obstacles big and small. What rebuilt my courage and showed me the inner core of strength that I always had, was returning to martial arts training. Doing something that was my passion, where I felt good about myself, was accepted and where I was tested in training and grading situations and found I had what it took, re-built my self-confidence and gave me courage. Once you find courage in a big situation and take action, it will be easier to act in similar situations in the future. You will find yourself flexing that courage muscle in all sorts of everyday problems such as taking steps to seek out a new and better job, challenging yourself to compete in a fun run, trying to reconnect with an isolated family member. There is courage in a myriad of everyday situations, big and small.

Courage requires us to not limit ourselves, to look outside whatever situation we are in and see something more, something greater, something better for ourselves or others. It is taking a chance to change something, to move forward to step into the unknown. Courage is built from a foundation of knowledge that we can do more, be more, deserve more, so we take the leap.

> "You gain strength, courage and confidence by every experience in which you really stop to look fear in the face. You are able to say to yourself, *'I have lived through this horror. I can take the next thing that comes along.'* You must do the thing you think you cannot do." — Eleanor Roosevelt

SEEING THE OPPORTUNITY

To approach life positively, to see what is possible, you need to execute some mindset shifts.

The way we think of and approach adverse situations that occur comes from experience, learned thought patterns and beliefs. These are deep-seated within our subconscious, and we need to consciously act to recognize and change them over time.

Every situation presents us with an opportunity to learn and to grow. If we are willing to learn, then we can grow and become better people. Not only can we become better, but we can be an example and teach others to become better too.

We have a choice to respond in a way that is negative, which will keep us stuck in the problem, or we can respond with positivity.

We can learn what we did right, what worked, what plan we can follow when next in that situation. We can pass this positive plan on to our children as an example for them to follow if they ever face a similar problem.

We can also look at what did not work, what reaction was not successful but in a positive way. To do this, we need to look at what didn't work objectively, without feeling bad about ourselves or apportioning blame. Instead, we need to recognize what didn't work and ask ourselves what we can learn, what we could have done differently, what would have been a better response.

Only in embracing the problem with positivity, seeing it as an opportunity, being willing to seek the answers within can we solve it.

EMBRACING THE JOURNEY

Opportunities in life open up every day if we dare to look, if we are open to them and notice the world around us, what is being said to us, what connections are being made. So many people go through life with their eyes closed, never daring to think that there can be more, never seeing the window of opportunity opening in front of them.

So the saying goes, everything happens for a reason - it truly does.

My journey in life to this point has seen me lose and re-discover myself, seen me combat and survive a long-term toxic relationship while running a busy law firm and raising two boys, seen me discover the unexpected gifts of learning and teaching martial arts, seen me be a mother, sister, daughter, auntie, friend, mentor, teacher.

Doing all of that has shown me my purpose in life: to share the lessons I have learned, and coach and mentor women who exist in the same stressful and toxic world I used to inhibit so that they too can find the way out. Not everyone is as fortunate as I have been to navigate my way out and have the support in doing so.

So my journey from here is to bring the light and lessons for all those women out there who need me, and I know that there are thousands of them. This is part of why I am sharing my story in the hope that they might see that there is light and a way forward.

I can only do that because I have now travelled far enough to embrace the whole journey. Perspective is a powerful thing, and I am grateful for all of it because I now have the tools, resources and ability to help others, such a blessing.

GRATITUDE

The most powerful state of being is gratitude.

Gratitude can help you find that chink of light.

When we are in the middle of a crisis, because our perspective has been altered, we can forget that we have so many things to be grateful for. No matter what your situation, you can find something to be thankful for.

You might be living in a tumultuous domestic situation, but you can be grateful for a hug or a kiss from your children. Thankful for your dog that wags his tail when he sees you. The feel of the warmth of the sun on your back as you hang out the washing, even if it is the 4th load you have hung out today—the blue of the sky, the beauty of the sunset.

These small things, if you look for them, can sustain you. They are the chink of light in the darkness that can show you there is a way out. It is there in the distance, but you can get there. Sometimes they can be hard to see, but if you look, there is always something there.

This was me, my escape was walking my dog every day, often twice a day, because it allowed me to escape my prison, to let my mind some space to unwind and unclench a little, and I was grateful for the breeze on my face, for the crunch of the frost at my feet, for the warmth of the sun. Walking sustained me, and I was grateful for every walk I went on every day. I was thankful for any time he was out of the house, and we could relax for however short a time. This was how I survived.

It was a day-to-day existence being grateful for the small things.

Now that my life has transformed, there is so much more to be grateful for each day. I am thankful for the richness and expansiveness of my new life, for all the unique experiences and things I have achieved in just four short years, so many that I could write another book. I am grateful for all of the wonderful friends from all over the world that I have made in that time, grateful for my amazing family's love and support, grateful that I am free and independent and live an extraordinary life of joy, happiness, love and abundance.

Grateful that I am now able to impact the lives of others in such a positive way right here in this book, in my coaching and teaching. By setting an example of what is possible, what can be overcome and how you can truly transform yourself from being a squashed and damaged soul hiding from the world, into someone vibrant, alive and open to all that life has in store.

I am incredibly grateful for the whole of my life journey, good and bad, because it has made me who I am. It has made me strong, resilient, courageous, confident, compassionate, accepting, open, loving, and happy. It has made me a leader, a light-bringer for others to show them the way. It has taught me not to be afraid to be vulnerable, that I don't need to be perfect, that I am unique and just being fully me, who I am right now is more than enough.

Burning down my former life, choosing to change, being willing to do the work each day no matter how hard, being willing to look within and see the answers, to keep taking the steps has transformed me into who I am now and who I am yet to be.

A phoenix has risen from the ashes and is now able to fly.

ME.

JENNIFER GASKELL

"A girl should be two things: who and what she wants." — Coco Chanel

Jennifer Gaskell is the CEO and Founder of Pink Palm MarCom and the co-founder of the Durham Women's Network, a group of more than 5,000 inspirational and connected women leaders on the eastern border of Toronto.

With nearly 20 years of experience in the public relations field, Jennifer has dedicated her career to promoting and marketing local businesses and entrepreneurs. She has also committed significant time in her career to public service.

Jennifer has pivoted her life and career in numerous ways within the last 12 months to follow her dreams and support the women within her network as they experienced the fallout of the COVID-19 pandemic.

In the fall of 2019, she enrolled at Trent University to complete an Honours Degree in Communications; and, in the summer of 2020, she created her own communications agency, Pink Palm MarCom.

This community influencer is a master collaborator, networker, cheerleader and intuitive coach who generously gives her time to mentor numerous women. Her ambition for creative project management has led her to develop numerous business opportunities for herself.

Her work with the Durham Women's Network has resulted in many successful events, such as the wellness/business hybrid retreat re:Create 2020 and an annual Holiday Gift Guide encouraging the community to shop local. Since launching in 2019, the group has grown exponentially. High profile partnerships with worldwide brands, such as Sandals Resorts, and Eat Travel Rock are driving future networking initiatives.

Jennifer firmly believes in the strength of finding your business niche and aligning with the right clients. She values being a positive female role model and takes the initiative to mentor others in the communications field.

FROM AUTOPILOT TO AUTHENTIC: HOW I STARTED LISTENING TO MYSELF AND BUILT A COMMUNITY OF SUPPORT

BY: JENNIFER GASKELL

As I sit in my den, a cup of coffee in hand and writing my deepest thoughts, I realize how full my life is and feel gratitude. It's taken me 38 years to get here, and I've learned many lessons along the way. I can intuitively feel an exciting path ahead; I've given myself permission to let go and follow it. That path is no longer scary because I have a support system—something that I never fully had before. And, I have boundaries, something I had never implemented before.

Have you ever felt like your biggest successes come after a period of intense uncertainty and scrutiny? I think that some people are innately focused on creating a soft spot to land during hard times—that's me.

In the last five years—after going through a separation, family health issues and more—I feel like I've grown the most than in my previous thirty-something years on the planet.

A mid-career separation was the catalyst for massive changes taking me through many valleys and peaks. But for every valley it left me in—I still had the strength to wake up every morning and carry on. "Just keep swimming" (for those of you who know me well, I am a Disney fanatic.), and that's what I did. That one statement gave me the strength I needed to keep going even when I couldn't see the path ahead.

The shame of going through a divorce so early in life is like nothing else. I blamed myself, worried about my kids and how I would keep a roof over their heads. At the time, I had absolutely no self-awareness and didn't set aside time to take care of myself. But, I knew I had to put my chin up and keep going.

Carrying on meant I had to grow up in a completely different way—and quickly. By all means, I am not afraid of change. I've always been the one to change jobs, hairstyles, household paint colours with no stress. But this was different.

One of my girlfriends hit the nail on the head:

"Brave people can break out of the autopilot life and be authentic. That takes change. And most people are afraid of change."

Thank you, Carrie W.

Surviving financially (buying my own house!) and building my own routine was paramount to the confidence I was building in myself. But just as things would build to a peak, I would just as quickly tumble down. I'd think to myself, *what am I doing wrong*? I started to think about myself and worried about people talking about me, my career, and my family.

I gathered a lot of strength from looking inward. It helped me to not only heal but also lead. The great Brené Brown and her wise advice on leading from the heart, not hurt, demonstrates how this is possible.

At my lowest point, I must have been projecting my pain and suffering because there were times where others jumped on the opportunity to add more. It was especially harsh in the workplace, where I had put in more than a decade of hard work, sweat and love. Some whispered about me behind my back, *about my problems,* and those who openly judged me and made their own assumptions.

"She doesn't have a university degree and isn't qualified for her position."

...even though I had more than a decade of experience and a related three-year college diploma.

"She slept her way to the top."

Yes, they went there. I had a lot going on in my life and people wanted to connect the dots to villainize me so that there was a scapegoat for all the toxic problems going on in the workplace.

"She always needs to ask others to validate her opinion."

My collaborative personality seemed to get in the way of building positive relationships with others in management who took my openness as a weakness.

Those were the words that I heard in the workplace from other women who I thought were allies.

Although I'm an introvert, I could always easily adapt myself to social situations. However, I never had a full support network of female friends—the kind that gathered on Thursday nights for must-see TV or enjoyed an annual girls' trip. I didn't know what I didn't know. I now realize that I missed connections with other women. However, in my first marriage, I always had other priorities and never took the time for self-care. I felt guilty at the thought of spending time with friends sans children.

There were many lonely moments in my mid-thirties, and I'm not proud of myself for not asking for help. After a particularly hard year—losing my mentor at work and facing declining mental health due to the culture of intimidation there—I realized that I needed more. Many pieces of my life had fallen into place, but I needed a space to feel good about myself again. I visualized myself in a circle of women supporting me. This manifested itself into something bigger than I could have imagined.

Fast forward months later—the idea of the Durham Women's Network. It was my soft spot to land in a climate of uncertainty. I knew I had something in me to create instead of worrying and projecting my fears onto others. It has come at a time when I have found stability in my family life, with a partner (now husband) who is amazingly supportive. This new network was going to help drive the upward trajectory I was on.

The initial idea was a spark that entered my mind in 2019. I attended a local Chamber of Commerce event commemorating International Women's Day, and it made me think about how woman-to-woman support exists and needs to be more accessible. If I was feeling uncertain and needing help—surely someone else felt the same? I knew it was time to model the change that needed to happen.

I also happened to run into long-time friend Kerri King at the event, who had mentored me through the years. And after just a short day of some powerful discussions about significant changes in both of our lives, I had courage to share an idea with her—the Durham Women's Network.

What if… women could support other women like this. It is time to feel good enough, to let go of fears. I left the event feeling energized.

Kerri and I had worked closely together marketing Durham Region's arts and culture community and had developed significant relationships with female entrepreneurs during that time. By 2019, we were no longer working together, but we both found ourselves in similar places in life—divorced and looking for a sense of community and friendship. We launched the network in April of that year with an event that was pulled together in just a few short weeks.

The night before DWN launched, I was wracked with nerves. I had invited media, Whitby's prominent Federal

Member of Parliament, Celina Caesar-Chavannes, and a number of women. What if no one showed up? The anxiety was intense.

As I laid in bed pondering those questions, my phone pinged with a text. Kerri had sent me an urgent message. She had to rush to Sick Kids Hospital in Toronto with her son, who had a freak accident with a drinking glass. Shards of glass ended up in his eye after his cup crumbled like sand in his hand. I was now struck with worry for her, her son Jordan, and the pending event. There was no way she would be joining me.

I went to work in the morning and thought about my schedule, how I would pack up at 4:15 p.m. and make it to the restaurant by 4:30 p.m. allowing myself time to set up for the first-ever Durham Women's Network event. Oh, and putting on a fresh coat of lipstick and combing my hair too, changing into my dress and suede knee-high boots.

Throughout the day, I received messages from friends who heard what happened—and offered to meet me at The Brock House to set up. I realized I was blessed when many friends showed up early to help.

That night—three media outlets showed up—and 50 women! I was shocked. And nervous that the restaurant was going to look down on me for hosting a much bigger event than I had promised. They didn't. They were happy for all the business.

I made so many vital connections that night and renewed my sense of camaraderie with women.

The next morning, the news had started to drop all the stories of the new Durham Women's Network. I was elated and even more shocked to see women celebrating me. I'll never forget when Linda Flynn, the associate vice-president of Development and Alumni at Durham College, gave a shout-out to me on our Facebook group for a local article that ended up in the paper.

Why is she celebrating me? I wondered. *I don't even know her.*

But, I got to know Linda and learned about her through DWN. She was a graduate of the Durham College Public Relations program, like me, and a super successful, smart, articulate woman.

It was moments like that one where I felt some strong connections being made—and many more personal and professional ones have been developed since.

After the initial launch event, the network quickly grew and evolved into a full-scale community. At the time, Kerri and I used Facebook as a platform to bring attendees together for in-person events. I created the Facebook group on the social network—which started with a modest 100 women. By June, that number had grown to 2,000. After several successful events that saw women meeting up "in real life," the group went virtual due to the COVID-19 pandemic. Remaining connected during this time of uncertainty was a challenge. Today, the group of local women encompasses more than

5,000 members and includes women of all business and personal backgrounds.

I can believe in the success of this network because we needed it as women. My original expectations have been greatly exceeded—a testament to what it means to going with your gut, or as Kerri says, following your intuition.

Leading and being included in this digital community has been a positive aspect in the era of Coronavirus, at a time when connections are craved. In the past year, the group has travelled to Barbados, connected with now author Celina Caesar-Chavannes and conversed with various business experts—all virtually.

Why is it such a strong community? I ask myself this all the time. Multigenerational connections are made—women entering the workforce and retired women; new and expectant mothers and empty-nesters. The group aims to support and elevate women. Members connect to find answers to questions about careers, goals, personal matters and more. Virtual events, conversation threads, and general socialization are a proxy for human connection that is deeply desired. Mentorship is valued. Friendships are made at a time when it is not easy to do so—whether because of the pandemic or because of the nuances of making later-in-life friends.

As a result of this supportive environment, my life has become more positive. Has this all made me stronger? Yes. My life is slowly stabilizing to be assertive, kind and positioned for success. If you put out positivity into the world, it will come back to you. This is what you deserve—we all deserve it.

What I have come to realize is that my experience led me down an important journey to self-awareness. If I thought people were talking about me during my times of challenge—it was likely they were. Accepting that, and being in touch with my own emotions, whether or not they made me feel good, was necessary.

It also brought me to the realization that I had left out a lot from my life that I had to add back in.

Connecting with others. Understanding the needs of my children and how they viewed me as a role model gave me strength. My friends were a force field for me, and I could not be where I am today without them. As an introvert—connecting with others can take energy from me. But I am learning how to replenish my energy stores and maintain relationships at the same time.

The power of touch. A hand on my shoulder, a hug, a kiss; it all went so far in providing me with what I needed to carry on.

Scheduling time for self-care. Not waiting to need it. Being able to put the oxygen mask on myself so I can care for others. We put so much effort into maintenance for everything else – cars, house, why not ourselves? This means—going to the spa; exercise; listening to music; creating art—the pieces of our identity that need tending to maintain who we are.

Sleep. I can't emphasize enough how much I value it. Perhaps one day I'll write a book entirely on the power of sleep. It truly resets us and gives us the capacity to think clearly and be well, physically and mentally.

Reconnecting with nature. Experience the sounds of running water, birds, trees, silence. It soothes your soul and recharges you for the real world.

Getting out of my comfort zone with new experiences. It helps to prepare you for change that will inevitably come your way. It exercises your ability to deal with the unknown on your own terms.

Travelling. Feel the exhilaration of breathing in new air and taking in new sights and sounds. This is not always easy with so many responsibilities but it can be as easy as camping out an hour from home for a night under the stars.

I know that the journey is still ongoing—there is no rush from me to get to a destination. I have opened a new book in my life, and I intend to write this amazing story on my own accord. One that puts me in charge of designing my life.

The DWN was a light bulb moment for me. I have met some of the most inspiring women through this network—some who were new to the area and looking for friends, others who were keen on making business connections. It was a true contrast between the negative environment I had become trapped in at work and the petty competition about who was receiving a promotion and why. Durham Women's Network was the umbrella I needed to get me through a storm. I look back at my story and sometimes think to myself that this would never have happened without my hurdles. It was because of the obstacles that I rose above—and transformed myself in the process. When you've been through what you think is the worst you can go through, you realize how tough you are. For me, it relieved my fears and anxieties. It allowed me to open myself to new opportunities. It gave me the strength to manifest everything I ever wanted in my life.

In case you are wondering. I finally left that job. I applied and was accepted to university to complete a degree. I found others who valued my love of collaboration. I started my own businesses. I got married to the love of my life.

And this time, I know what I need to succeed.

It's time to shine on.

KATE LESSLIE

Kate Lesslie is a devoted single mumma bear who is raising her two free thinking bear cubs and mischievous English Staffy in a quaint little townhouse on the Sunny Coast of Queensland, Australia.

She loves her pyjamas, Chris Cornell, eating vegan ice cream out of the tub, and has a long-standing obsession with children's books.

Kate could have already written multiple bestselling books over the course of her life… however, her debilitating fear of not being 'good enough', along with the myriad of other irrational fears and limiting beliefs she held, had always stopped her from ever publishing anything or moving beyond the cupboards full of scribbled on notepads and bench-tops covered with untouched scripts of truly enriching, and equally hilarious, liquid gold…. That is, until now!

Kate is an inspirational modern-day example of the true power conscious transformation can have on one's life.

With over 20 years of experience in the early childhood and education sectors and as a now veteran unschooling mumma who definitely prefers to live 'outside the box', Kate is an advocate for raising children as valued, autonomous, empowered human beings.

Through combining her innate affinity with children, her background studying and applying transformational mindset coaching, her passion for living an autonomous lifestyle and her natural ability to intuitively connect with children and parents on a relatable and vulnerable level, it's not at all surprising that she has organically landed in the magical combined role of 'Unschooling Coach' and 'Storyteller'.

Through her group coaching programs, and her 'Liberated Life Learner' membership for unschooling parents, Kate is helping 'new to unschooling' parents to break away from the mainstream schooling systems and adopt a much more liberated, free-thinking, 'out of the box' approach that completely transforms the way parents and their children embark on the learning journey called 'Life'.

Kate believes one of the quickest ways to connect with and enrich a child's heart is to bring laughter and joy into their world which is why she is currently working on her debut children's book series 'The Wilderness'. Her intention is to use her storytelling superpowers and witty Aussie humour to create books that empower, educate, and entertain children all across the world.

She can be found where most people are found these days… on social media (yes, she gradually buckled and found her way back online after her extremely satisfying year off socials!)

Kate is going to share the powerful changes her life has gone through. Transformations so meaningful that she can only express them in the strongest of terms. So, get ready because the F-bombs are coming in her chapter!

Instagram: @katelesslie_unschoolingcoach

Facebook: @Kate Lesslie Unschooling-Coach

Website: www.katelesslie.com

COURAGE LEADS TO FREEDOM

BY: KATE LESSLIE

I took a year.

You know how high-schoolers take a year after they finish school, and they go to some completely isolated, off-the-beaten-track village to do character-building volunteer work, building schools for underprivileged children? Or they go off to some sexy European country to drink beer for a year and say they've gone to 'find themselves'?

Well, I'm not a high-schooler; in fact, it's been over 20 years since I left high school, and although I've done plenty of volunteer work over the years, I've never built a school, and I don't like beer, but I took a year. I definitely didn't go to a sexy European country. In fact, I barely left my suburb and rarely got out of my pyjamas… but I took a year—a year doing something most people would probably find more challenging than building a school in an isolated village. Sadly, most people between the ages of 13-45 would spiral into debilitating anxiety at just a hint of what I did; experiencing withdrawal symptoms likened to that of an addict coming down off their drug of choice. Are we all really that addicted?

I took a year.

A year away from social media!

So, I deleted socials, among other things, from my phone and from my world for a year, and during that year, A LOT of shit went down in my world, a lot of positive, or you could even say *magical* shit.

When I stepped away from the onslaught of the ego-driven, fear-based energy that permeates into our minds on a daily basis via news feeds and notifications, there was a surprising amount of time for soul alignment, standing in my power, creating boundaries, neutralising my fear-based energy, and allowing inner peace to flow. It was during this time, I came to realise that throughout the course of my entire life, there had been ONE common denominator keeping me 'trapped'...

Let's point out the totally obvious thing that holds *soooooooooooo* many of us back from living our DREAMS, and from living our TRUTH.

Keeps us from LIVING. OUR. FUCKING. LIVES!

♬ Let's talk about FEAR baby,

Let's talk about you and me,

Let's talk about all the 'REAL' things

And the ILLUSIONS that may be ....

Let's talk aboouut FEAR! ♬

*(haha the Salt-'N-Pepa fans will get it ♬)

FEAR.

Fucking Fear.

Fear of judgment, abandonment and rejection.

Fear of inadequacy, being deeply loved or unconditionally loving oneself.

Fear of trusting oneself, of failure or success.

Fear of change, losing control or being alone.

Fear of confrontation or upsetting others.

Fear of starting a business.

Fear of going to sleep, the dark or the unknown.

Fear of driving long distances, or outside of your neighbourhood.

Fear of dogs, or literally any animal with fur or hair. To the point where you won't date or visit anyone who owns a pet or even *sit* somewhere if an animal sat there first!

Oops, I may have gotten carried away there and just started rattling off the fears that I allowed to control *my* life for almost 40 years!

To be honest, I think I had more fear coursing through my veins than the Hulk had gamma radiation coursing through his!

But I'm sure about 99% of you would be able to relate to at least something on my list?

Am I right??

So, A LOT of life-altering shifts occurred, in ridiculously positive, magical ways.

There was A LOT of silence, which is pretty much guaranteed to be ridiculously positive (and magical). By 'silence' I mean the kind of peaceful silence that comes from just stopping. From disconnecting from all the unnecessary external noise, stepping away from all the group chats, instant messaging, mindless scrolling, hashtags, notification pings, constant reminders, and the 'to-do' lists.

By the way, there's a big difference between dedicating your time and energy to what I like to call the *have-to-do* list when you could instead be creating a *want-to-do* list.

A quick life hack there.

I swapped my '*have*-to-do' life list for a '*want*-to-do' life list and it was liberating AF.

How you might ask?

Well, that story goes back a little further than just one year. My want-to-do life was ignited the day I stood in my power and advocated for my eldest child by taking him out of the mainstream schooling system to embark upon the liberating journey of unschooling.

Years of conditioning and living to the expectations of others had me believing I HAD to live life a certain way, HAD to follow certain rules, HAD to live a life that made others feel comfortable, even though it made me, the real me, fall further away from my truth. My heart used to ache. It ached to find a way to help my child through something I thought I had no control over and no way out of, because I had been conditioned by society to believe that to be true.

My heart ached because I thought I HAD to keep sending my child back to school day after day even though he would be begging me through gut-wrenching tears each morning not to make him go!

I thought I HAD to keep sending him even though I disagreed with the values and beliefs he was being indoctrinated with day in, and day out, by strangers who clearly didn't share the same values as I did.

I thought I HAD to send him even though I knew with every fibre of my being that it was traumatising and crushing his soul because he was being bullied not only by students but also by *teachers*. Yes, I moved him to another school but it was equally as bad.

My heart was aching.

It was through witnessing my first born, an imprint of my own heart, becoming merely another statistic in the rat-race of the 'have-to lifestyle' and a slave to living to the expectations and limiting beliefs of others that I realised something must change.

Enough was enough, nothing was worth seeing my child like that day after day and nothing was worth allowing an outdated, constrictive, over conditioned, fear-based society dictate our every move.

I made a conscious choice to start living my *own* life in my *own* way.

This mumma bear took a stand.

Even though it SERIOUSLY ruffled some feathers within my family…it was from that day, that decision, and that reclaiming of power, that my want-to life was ignited and as a family, our empowered journey into 'life without school' began.

The unschooling journey quite quickly proved itself to be so much more than simply living without school, it was the catalyst for an entire paradigm shift, one in which has opened doors to friendships, connections, enlightened perspectives, understandings and discoveries that could never be replaced or forgotten.

Once you experience this newfound level of liberated awareness and freedom and are able to see the world through the autonomous eyes of an 'unschooler', there really is no going back to life as you once knew it.

It simply wouldn't be possible, but also, why on earth would you even want to?

The only regret is why didn't I do it sooner! But unfortunately, I was one of those people who had never even considered homeschooling.

I didn't even know it was a legal option!

I thought it was just for 'rule breaking, tree hugging hippies', people in religious cults or for the offspring of the famous Hollywood types who were either too busy jet setting around the world to bother with school or would get mobbed by fans if they ever went to school.

I sure as hell didn't know it was an option someone like me, (a non-famous, non-cult following, single, unemployed mum) could consider.

School is so heavily established within society and passed down through generations as THE ONLY pathway to succeed in life and that was no different in my family, so I never even thought to question it!

But…

I have since learnt; school does not equal education.

We are led to believe that we, as parents, are not smart enough, capable enough, qualified enough to teach our own children.

"I'm not smart enough to homeschool my child!"

"What about socialisation?!!"

"What if I fail and my kids are ruined for life?!"

"What about university!?"

I realised, I already *was* and always will be my children's first and best teacher, nobody will ever know or care about my children more than I do. Nobody will ever have my children's best interests at heart the way I do, and nobody will ever have as much interest in my children's passions as I do!

My children needed me to overcome my fears, stand in my power and show them that I am willing to defend them and advocate for them and for myself.

I had to let them see me step out of my comfort zone and take a chance to do something that scares me, something I hadn't done before, something I was unsure about.

I showed them that you can step outside the box and away from 'the norm', and out of the grasps of the expectations and demands of others.... especially when those expectations and demands are not to one's benefit.

I let them see me do all of this not only for them, but for myself.

My children have witnessed me face my fears and model to them that I can do hard things with ease and as a result of that conscious life transformation, we are now blissfully living our life like a trio of 80's rock stars. We do what we want, when we want and we don't answer to anybody! Ticking off the want-to-do life list one epic adventure at a time.

Now I'd ask you to consider this…

How many things on your 'have-to-do' list do you truly *have* to do?

How much of it could be more accurately categorised as people-pleasing or living to other people's expectations?

Those two questions alone embody a landslide of fears:

Fear of letting others down, often at the expense of your own happiness, time, effort, and sanity.

Fear of abandonment or rejection, "If I say No or 'go against the grain', will they leave or reject me?'

Fear of criticism or not being liked, "If I say No, or speak my truth maybe they will gossip about me or think I'm being selfish and won't like me anymore?"

Fear of conflict/confrontation and anger, "If I say No, or choose not to comply, will they be upset/disappointed/angry with me?".

The word 'No' is one of the first things we teach our children (and even our pets).

'Can I get this new toy?'

'No.'

So easy and automatic when talking to our children (and even those four-legged furry children) and yet for so many of us, the entire concept of the word seems to go straight out the window when it comes to being able to advocate for ourselves, create healthy boundaries and tell our parents, partners, friends or co-workers 'No.'

And just a friendly and empowering reminder to consider using 'No' as a complete sentence. You don't need to justify your answer or explain yourself… you can simply say 'No.' Yes, *even* to your overbearing, interfering, judgmental mother-in-law!

When you live to the expectations of others and to please others, you are ultimately basing *your* life choices on the external validation and approval of *others*. You are allowing the wants, needs, and desires of *other* people to override your own. You are neglecting *your* freedom, *your* happiness, *your* values, *your* beliefs, and openhandedly passing over your power on a silver platter purely to chase what others think of you and what society deems as 'success.'

Taking back your power and creating boundaries around your *want*-to-do list is a simple change that is empowering and completely life-altering!

Now, I'm not a brain surgeon or a rocket scientist.

Never given a TED talk, although, people who know me also know that most of my phone conversations are equally as long!

To be honest, debilitating anxiety and depression, as a highly undesirable undertone of living with dermatilomania disorder, kept me housebound for days, weeks, and even months at a time for a good part of 35 years.

For those who don't know what dermatilomania is, Google it because honestly, it would need an entire book of its own to be able to go into the depths of what it is and what it means to live with it.

It is more commonly known as 'chronic skin-picking disorder,' and anyone who has lived with dermatilomania knows to the core of their soul how it feels to endure.

The recurring spiral of shame, guilt, and embarrassment that haunts you as a result of it, had been one of the key elements that from the ripe old age of three, kept me trapped, stuck, and hidden away in what can only be described as the lonely hollows of hell.

With the unwavering list of fears combined with an entire lifetime of living ensnared by the impenetrable grasp of dermatilomania…

I thought I was broken and in CONSTANT need of 'fixing.'

I thought I was a monster—a broken, out-of-place, unlovable monster.

I always thought I was 'not enough.'

Not pretty enough, cool enough, or smart enough.

Not brave enough or strong enough.

And that is where I passively lived for most of my life.

Until…. I consciously transformed my life!

Now, here's where I could write a whole page worth of shoutouts to all the people who have guided me and supported me along my journey, but they all already know who they are and that would take a chapter of its own. They all know I have nothing but love and gratitude for them all.

They also know that even with ALL the guidance and support IN THE WORLD, I couldn't have transformed my life without the single most imperative ingredient…

ME!

Even with an overflowing toolbox full of tools created to guide, support, encourage, uplift, and enhance your life…

YOU are always the key ingredient!

You can read all the books, take all the courses, listen to all the podcasts, sign up for a promising new webinar each week…but it's all just noise.

Constantly grabbing at the external and needing MORE!

More courses, more podcasts, more books, more audios, more googling, more scrolling, more planning, more posting, more tweeting, and more questions.

What if I told you that ALL of that grabbing was actually your fear-based energy?

What do I mean by 'fear-based energy'? I quite simply mean any emotions that come under the 'fear' umbrella. You may recognise some of these old chestnuts…. worry, doubt, anxiety, frustration, jealousy, anger, shame, and guilt. I think you get the idea and I'm sure it would then come as no surprise that the love-based umbrella would cover emotions such as love, hope, honesty, respect, acceptance, passion, understanding, trust, forgiveness, harmony, gratitude, peace, confidence, and connection. That list could go on and on, but you get the idea, and I'm sure you can easily see how immeasurably different one's journey through life could be, even in the harshest of weather, depending on which umbrella they choose to take to protect themselves along their journey.

I wonder how different your world would feel if even just for one moment, those fear-driven energies, the grabbing, needing, and chasing…

STOPPED.

Now…

close your eyes and…

✨ breathe ✨

What if I told you that the one brief, blissful moment of inner peace that you just felt could become your new way of life?

Calm. Intentional. Peaceful.

No needy, fear-based energy fuelling your decisions and dictating your life.

I am living proof that it CAN be done, and if someone that was as deeply rooted in negative fear-based energy as I was can shift their ENTIRE way of life and overcome a list of fears that was longer than a 4-year-old's Christmas list…

ANYONE can!

I TACKLED EVERY SINGLE FEAR ON THAT LIST LIKE A WARRIOR GODDESS!!

And I did most of it without even getting out of my pyjamas.

Not kidding! It truly is THAT simple that you can do it without even taking off your dressing gown!

I even own a *dog* now!

This is the same person who, for her entire life, would have a fully-fledged internal freak out just from *seeing* dog hair on a seat!

Indeed that is an extreme transformation and since you may already be in disbelief that one person could be so fearful of something as seemingly harmless as pet hair, I'll take this opportunity to properly highlight the multi- level transformation that truly took place in that magical year. Remember I mentioned a fear of the dark, being alone and driving outside of the neighbourhood?

Well, that was no joke!

The fear of the dark had been life-long and even taking the garbage out alone at night was something that I just didn't do, even well into adulthood!

Being alone in a house at night? Hell no! Not even an option!

Driving on highways or long distances? Don't even bother asking.

Then how did I shift that fear and end up living the liberated hippieshake vanlife, travelling with just my kids along the East Coast of Australia in a motorhome, dragging the overflowing toilet cassette through dark and stormy caravan parks in the middle of the night... without any fear?

It was quite simple actually.

I stopped feeding the fears.

I finally realised the truth behind the saying 'fear is an illusion' and I created an empowering mantra for myself: 'Courage Leads to Freedom'. Then I simply focused my energy on everything I wanted that was on the other side of all of those fears!

Every 'fear' that I had *told* myself was real…. I simply dismissed. Any and all of my old limiting beliefs that were no longer serving me were rewritten to create a narrative that *did* serve me.

There is so much power in the stories we tell ourselves. So why not make them stories that are actually going to empower and enrich your life… It really does make life much more fun that way!

Oh, and remember, I managed to do all of this as a single mumma with next to zero money in my bank account and while unschooling my two kids.

Now I'm not saying that to get sympathy points or to look like a martyr. I'm simply wanting to give hope to anyone who may be feeling that there is no hope. If I can transform my life, ***you* can too**!

I know first-hand how it feels trying to live to the expectations of others rather than living YOUR truth!

I know how it feels to live captive to your fear-based energy.

I know how it feels to live small and safe and never step outside your comfort zone.

I know how it feels to let people walk all over you and allow them to tear down your boundaries and stomp on your values out of fear of the slightest confrontation or fear of upsetting others.

I know how it feels to resist what you KNOW your soul is truly craving because you feel that you are undeserving of true aligned happiness, because you feel undeserving of that 'dream life'... but most of all because you FEAR what would happen if you ACTUALLY got all that you desired.

Too good to be true?

You might be asking, "Why can others manifest whatever they want so easily but nothing ever quite works out for me?"

"If I could just get that new job/house/car… then I will finally be happy but (insert excuse here…)"

Sound familiar?

Now, many of you may have caught onto the fact that this way of thinking *does not* serve you but I want you to *believe* it, *know* it, and *trust* at a core level not only that you *are* deserving of all that you desire, but that you can manifest *all* that you desire… and it can be easy… if you allow it to be easy!

Experience speaks volumes, and I've been through the seasoned gates of hell and back...multiple times!

It's as though I was stuck in a revolving door where anxiety, depression, co-dependency, struggle and FEAR had me hooked on a loop and were welcoming me back with open arms and a slimy grimace every time.

As painful as it was, I now know that each part was orchestrated by my soul in order to guide me closer to my aligned path. Even the shitty parts that felt as though my heart and soul were ripping from my body.

Those parts were actually my soul screaming at me that I was out of alignment with my authentic truth.

But my experiences and the knowledge I gained by trekking through the shadowy, dark parts of my journey can now help my own children so that they don't have to go through the same painful, drawn-out and confusing path that I went through buckling to fear and the expectations of others.

I know now that I have the tools and the strength to help guide my children and allow them to grow and experience their *own* journey, to model to them how to neutralise their fear-based energy, to stand empowered and advocate for themselves and to live *their* truth. To help them reach that place of inner and outer autonomy all the while guiding them closer to their authentic truth in creating their own want-to-do life, whatever that may look like for them.

There is a powerful message here for all:

Courage leads to freedom. When you learn to trust yourself, trust your strength,

stand in your power and advocate for yourself, you are telling the universe and everyone around you that you are ready to LIVE. YOUR. OWN. LIFE....and that you are a force to be reckoned with!

I KNOW this because I did it and I continue to do it every day.

Imagine living a life you don't need a vacation from!

That's what a life that is fully aligned and authentically YOU can feel like!

That inner knowing like I had, that is your intuition, it's your soul guidance...and it's NEVER WRONG.

Acknowledge it.

It knows.

YOU know.

You will know when you are feeling called and when your soul is ready to evolve higher and to make that permanent paradigm shift into authentic alignment and trust me, it IS permanent. Once you reach a new level of consciousness and awareness, it's simply impossible for you to go back to your old mindset and old way of living. Your world WILL change for the better and you will not even recognise the old you!

Believe me...once you start the 'everything you've always desired' relationship with yourself, and start living your want-to-do life, you won't ever go back to that shitty, undervalued, disconnected, unaligned relationship you offered yourself or the have-to-do life you settled for in the past. And as an added bonus, purely by default, once you have that level of relationship with *yourself*, it's simply then a matter of the 'law of attraction' that the universe must then match that which you are vibrating into the universe.

Make sure you are sending off some seriously epic vibes and watch the magic truly start to unfold in your life.

Courage leads to freedom.

So, ignite that courage and go LIVE. YOUR. FUCKING. LIFE.

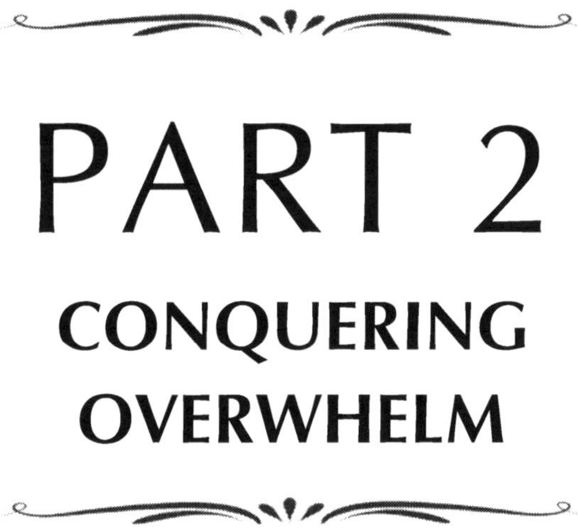

PART 2
CONQUERING OVERWHELM

LINDSAY COUTURE

Lindsay Couture is a caregiver, coach, and woman business owner. When she's not working in the office, caring for people or spending time with her mom, you can find her in the forest surrounded by nature, out kayaking, or in the gym lifting weights, refilling her own cup back up!

Owner of Oakwood Home Healthcare, Personal Support Worker, and advocate for both Caregivers and P.S.W's Lindsay became a caregiver for her mom at the early age of 11. She has supported her mom through respiratory issues and two double lung transplants. Caregiving is all she knows. Lindsay graduated from the PSW program in 2016 at the age of 21.

After caring for her mom and working in healthcare taking care of other people and their needs, Lindsay started to experience the effects of burnout. This burnout went on 6 months before she finally had to walk away from her career. During her time off Lindsay's mom went through her second double-lung transplant which ended up being Lindsay's catapult for change.

Now at the age of 28, Lindsay realizes why she went through all that darkness, she has turned her experiences into being a guiding light for others.

OVERCOMING CAREGIVER BURNOUT

BY: LINDSAY COUTURE

Have you ever put the needs of someone else before yours to the point where you neglected even your most basic needs? As a family caregiver and a Personal Support Worker, everyone else's needs were always my priority. My own somehow got pushed to the backburner. That is what led me down the path of complete burnout.

Rock bottom. That is where I was. Back in the summer of 2018, I can remember feeling so disgusted with myself. I had gained 100 pounds, neglected my mental health, and I was on disability because I couldn't manage a job. This is how I had lived for a year. My days didn't consist of much. I stayed home most of the time. I ate an unbelievably huge amount of junk food and I remember often thinking that this was going to be my life - for the rest of my life. I became accustomed to this lifestyle. This was my comfort zone.

It was December 3, 2018 that changed my life forever. I can remember my mom calling me, "Lindsay, they have lungs; we have to be in Toronto for four". This is a phone call I've received five other times before. This was my mom's second double-lung transplant, and before this call, we had already experienced the let-down of two false calls because the lungs weren't good enough to be transplanted.

I headed home to help my mom prepare for our trip to Toronto. I thought she'd be nervous, but to my surprise, she wasn't — the previous false calls had made her lose hope. We got her belongings together and packed up the car. We began our trip down Highway 401 to Toronto General Hospital.

When we arrived, it was the usual same old song and dance. We got her registered, headed to get a chest x-ray, and then headed up to the seventh floor – the transplant floor. The nurses greeted us with huge smiles. Before I go on, I must say – the nurses at Toronto General Hospital are the best. They are the most kind, compassionate and skilled.

We were shown to my mom's room. I switched her from the oxygen tank to the wall hook-up, and the nurses began their assessment. Time seemed to be moving so slow. The whole time we waited, it didn't seem real. I was waiting for a doctor to enter the room with the look of disappointment on their face, to tell us the lungs were no good, and we would be sent on our way like we had the two times before.

But to my surprise – no doctor. Just the odd nurse to check vitals, or a quick visit to ensure my mom was comfortable. The set time for the transplant was 1 AM. But 1 AM came and left, so did 2 AM. The nurses kept coming in to tell us there was a delay. I thought this transplant was never going to happen. At 3 AM, the nurses came in the room to put the compression stockings on my mom – *this was new*. I volunteered to put the stockings on my mom.

I got the compression stockings on. A nurse came in to let us know there would be a porter here shortly to take my mom to the operating room. *The operating room??? Was this really happening?* A flood of emotion hit me. I went from calm and relaxed to extremely anxious. My mom and I are best friends; it's been just her and me for most of my life. I've been my mom's primary caregiver since the age of 11. Ever since then, our relationship has grown in ways that many people wouldn't understand. The fact that she was about to go in for her second double-lung transplant scared the hell out of me. I knew the complications the second time around posed a greater risk – I was scared I would never see her alive again.

The porter arrived to my mom's room. I unhooked her from the wall oxygen and hooked her back up to the oxygen tank. We began our walk to the elevator, my family followed along. We got into the elevator and rode it down to the second floor. The whole time my heart was racing. All I wanted to do was cry – but I knew I had to stay strong for my mom. We said our goodbyes, and it took all the strength inside of me not to break down. I said, "I love you, Mom." She replied with "love you, Lindsay," and that's when they wheeled her through the doors to the Operating Room. I felt so numb; I didn't know what to think.

I was exhausted. It was now 4 AM. We were taken to a family waiting area. That's where we waited until 7 AM. I forget now if I slept or not; that part is all a blur. At 7 AM, we moved to another waiting area where you could receive updates regarding your loved one in the operating room. At noon, there was still no update on my mom. My mom's last transplant only took 7 hours. After the 7 hours, she rested comfortably in the ICU for a few days before downgrading to the stepdown unit, making it home within two weeks.

So, at 12 PM, I approached the lady at the desk and asked her if there was any update regarding my mom. She asked me to hold on while she phoned down to the O.R. There was no answer. My stomach felt uneasy. I went and sat back down with my family. When 2 PM came, I approached the desk again. It had been 10 hours since my mom went into the O.R. I asked the lady if there was any update. She called down to the O.R. Still no answer. *Was her heart okay? Were there bleeding complications?* I said to the lady, "You need to please call back down there and get me an update! That's my mom, my best friend and I need to know she's alright." The lady picked the phone up and dialed back down to the O.R. Finally, an answer. All they could say was that they couldn't afford to lose anyone from the O.R at the moment to update the family, but they were able to tell the lady that they were just putting the second lung in. *Only just putting the second lung in? It's been 10 hours.*

I continued to wait in that waiting room until around 8 PM. My family thought it'd be best if I went home to get some rest while she was still in surgery. Even though I didn't want to leave the hospital, I knew that this would be the only time I had to sleep in the days to come. I got home around 9 PM, and it was 10 PM when I received the phone call that she was out of the O.R and waiting to be transported to the ICU. I got on the phone with my family and asked to be driven back to the hospital.

I arrived back at the hospital and headed up to the waiting room on the 10th floor, where families can wait while their loved ones are in the ICU. To get to see your loved one in the ICU, you need to phone the nurse assigned to them to get the okay to come in. When I got there, I called into the reception and asked to be transferred to my mom's nurse. The nurse gave me the okay, so I went in. What I was about to see will be forever ingrained into my mind as one of my worst memories.

I got to my mom's room, and I walked in. There she was lying in the hospital bed. She was hooked up to so many machines. She had I.V. lines and drain tubes everywhere. My mom was swollen; she didn't look anything like herself. The nurses still hadn't cleaned her up, so bloody gauze pads came out of her nose and mouth alongside her ventilator. Her eyes were still taped shut. I was scared. Immediately, I broke down. The tears came flooding down my face. I'm surprised I didn't fall to the floor. I held my mom's hand, and I told her I loved her.

The next 24 hours proved to be challenging. I received a phone call from the hospital explaining to me that my mom had to go back into the O.R due to bleeding complications. Her chest tube kept filling up with blood overnight and they needed to bring her back to the O.R to fix the problem. To do this, the hospital needs consent from the Power of Attorney; I gave my consent. Three hours went by, they got the bleeding under control, and she was on her way back to the ICU for close monitoring.

During this time, well even before the transplant had happened, I was in a bad place mentally. I can remember sitting at home thinking my mom wasn't going to survive. I contemplated taking my life numerous times, the only reason I didn't was because my mom was still here. *If my mom doesn't make it, I hope my family is prepared to bury both of us.* I knew I had nothing without my mom, so really – what was the point of living if she had died?

The following morning I attended the meeting with the surgical team in the ICU, my mom had now been out of the O.R from the initial surgery for just over 48 hours. They had every type of specialist as part of this discussion, the surgeon, his fellow, a medication team, two respiratory therapists, and three ICU nurses. I can remember the doctor fearing my mom's heart being damaged from being out of her chest for so long, *but only time would tell.* The next day, they had plans to start lowering her sedation to start the process of waking her up.

Waking up my mom while still intubated was one of her worst fears. During her first transplant, she didn't require the support of the ventilator any longer, and it was out before she was fully cognitive and back to her normal self. (The medications are heavy-duty, and often patients don't remember much right after transplant) I knew that the following day was going to be interesting when they lowered the sedation, but I never thought she would react like this.

I went home that day, and still, the thoughts of suicide crossed my mind. I was already at such a low point in my life. This had put me so close to ending it all. My mom continued to be my reason to hold on. My family encouraged me to come over and spend time with them, but I just wanted to be alone.

The following day I showed up at the hospital bright and early because I knew they were planning to lower the sedation in hopes of waking her up. I got to the 10th floor and called my mom's nurse. She gave me the okay, and I went in. My mom looked the same as the day before. But much better than when she first came out of the O.R. At first, she was full of fluid thus making her swollen. Once they started her on diuretics, the fluid came off quickly, and she returned to her normal body weight. After I was there for about an hour, they decided it was time to reduce the sedation medication.

It didn't happen immediately, but I could tell my mom was becoming agitated. She began moving her hands, and suddenly, her blood pressure started to climb; it got to 200/190 before the nurse made the decision to sedate her again. My heart broke, I knew it was my mom's anxiety, but I never thought it was going to react that badly.

The following day and the day after, they tried the same thing, and unfortunately, got the same reaction. The agitation, her blood pressure skyrocketing to 200/190, and sedation medication being re-administered. This seemed to become the routine. Putting her heart under this much pressure started to become dangerous. Later on the third day of trying, I noticed something wasn't right in her mouth. The ventilator was in there, the vent suction tube was in there – that pulls moisture and phlegm from the throat, and there was this other little tube I could see, but not identify.

I asked the nurse to come over. I showed her the tube and asked her what it was - she looked more confused than me. It turns out my mom's NG tube, which enters through your nose and is supposed to go to your stomach, was somehow coiled into her mouth. The nurse got the doctor who then ordered an X-ray. The doctor was happy with the placement of the NG tube in my moms' stomach, and because she was still so fragile after the surgery, he didn't want to change anything. **I knew** this was why my mom was reacting the way she was when they woke her up. The discomfort from this NG tube in her mouth probably made her feel like she was choking, which led her to panic. I told the nurse that something had to be done, but she had to follow the doctor's order.

The next morning, I called into the day nurse who was taking over my mom's care. I had told her my thoughts in regards to the misplacement of the NG tube, causing her to panic. The nurse *actually agreed (caregiver win)* and went ahead and fixed it regardless of what the order said. Later that day, we tried to lower her sedation again in hopes of success this time.

The nurse lowered the sedation. Soon after, my mom began to move her hands, but her heart didn't react the way it had the days before. This was progression in the right direction. Six days into recovery, and this was that first little bit of hope I'd been waiting for.

I'd visit my mom every single day until the ventilator came out. The ventilator stayed in for a week and a half. I can remember the first day it came out; hearing her say she loved me brought tears to my eyes, those three words I will never take for granted again. Never did I think she'd make it through this. She stayed in the ICU for another two days before being transferred down to the step-down unit. My mom was experiencing a lot of confusion and delirium at this point but I trusted their judgment call to transfer her.

I went to visit her the day they moved her to the step-down unit and was immediately concerned. She was placed in a ward with three other patients, and the nurses were busy tending to their needs. It had only been a week and a half since she had her transplant; the ventilator only had come out two days prior. To me, she was still very high needs. Being in bed so long, my mom's muscles became really weak, to the point where she was unable to walk and even stand on her own. With the delirium, she kept trying to get out of bed because she was adamant about "leaving the hospital to go home." The nurses could not supervise her, which made me nervous. The things she was saying made no sense; she was unable to form proper sentences. I left that day worried about her rapidly declining condition and her safety.

Later that evening, I got a phone call from the hospital. My mom's breathing became extremely laboured, and they had to put her back on the ventilator. They had come up with a diagnosis; she was septic. My heart broke. Working in healthcare, I know enough that when a diagnosis of sepsis is given usually the outcome is bad. I raced to the hospital; I even managed to get a speeding ticket along the way! There my mom was back in the ICU on life support fighting for her life. *Was this really happening? It all began to feel so surreal.* The doctors and nurses reassured me that they had started the antibiotics right away. *But was it enough?* Only time would tell.

Two days went by, and I felt so hopeless. My mom, my best friend, was fighting for her life, and I knew the one thing that kept her fighting was me. I would hold her hand and tell her I loved her. They say even though they are sedated, they can still hear you. I was hoping my voice was enough to keep her fighting. I knew she could hear me.

I am so thankful my mom responded well to the antibiotic treatment. It wasn't long, maybe two days before the ventilator came out, and she was breathing on her own again. After all the years I worked in long-term care, I'd never seen someone recover from sepsis. The delirium had subsided, and things began to progress forward again.

After spending four weeks at Toronto General Hospital, my mom was ready to be moved to Toronto Rehab to begin her other road to recovery. She had battled and made it through the surgical part of things – now it was time to start regaining her strength.

When my mom left Toronto General Hospital, she was still unable to stand. She had been in bed for four weeks, and their focus for the majority of that time was keeping her alive and healing the large wound on her chest, *not physiotherapy*. Toronto Rehab has a floor specifically for transplant patients, and this was the best next step in my mom's care.

I can remember the walk over to Toronto Rehab, through the underground tunnels and the elevators at Mount Sinai. Finally, we ended up at Toronto Rehab on the 4th floor, which turned into my mom's home for the next five weeks.

My mom progressed well. They had her doing physio twice daily, and all her meals were provided to her. I would come in to do her personal care during that time, and steal her from her unit to take her on wheelchair rides to the gift shops at Mount Sinai and Toronto General Hospital through the underground tunnels. It wasn't long before she began taking her own walks around the unit unsupervised. Finally, we had a discharge date in the foreseeable future, and this was something to look forward to!

During those two months, I had a lot of time to myself. For the first time in years, I had to learn how to be completely independent – as much as my mom depended on me, I relied on her for most things. It made me realize that if my mom had passed away, the reason I would have ended my life was because I thought I had nothing to live for. Not realizing that my purpose in life was exactly why I was living through that nightmare. Not just during those two months, but since an incredibly young age. I took on the roles and responsibilities of the primary caregiver for my mom. Even though I had mentioned previously that this made our relationship grow in ways that people wouldn't understand, it also changed the way I grew up. My obligations were different than most kids; I spent my time looking after my mom and attending her appointments. Most kids my age spent their time making friends, attending social events and going to school. My responsibilities even affected my ability to attend school. I had dropped out numerous times in high school because I couldn't handle the stress.

When my mom came home from Toronto Rehab, things shifted. I had this newfound motivation to make a change in my life. It started with my weight. During the two months my mom was in Toronto, I began losing weight due to stress, lack of eating and the amount of walking I did down there. The 20 pounds I lost during those two months was the fuel I needed to lose the 110 pounds I've lost since the day of my mom's initial hospitalization on Dec 3rd, 2018. The weight loss journey has been a whole lifestyle change. I had to change everything about my diet and exercise.

I started small. I stopped drinking pop and began walking around my neighbourhood. Just those two simple changes were enough for me to see the weight start to come off. Running was something I loved doing previous to my weight gain. But at 243 pounds, running was not an option. The shin splints I experienced were horrific, so I walked. I began to change my diet to healthier options, never resorting to a plate of lettuce and veggies because I knew that wasn't sustainable for me, and my risk for failure was close to 100%. I started to implement home workouts that I found on YouTube, finally feeling comfortable enough to step foot into a gym in July 2019.

My confidence slowly began to return, and I started to feel really good about myself and the progress I had made. I continued to work out for the rest of the summer, making it my number one priority. When the end of August came around, I was ready to start working again. I knew where my passion was – caring for people. But the last time I did this as a career, it put me in a place where I wanted to take my life. *How could I be a Personal Support Worker but on my own terms?* I put an ad up on Kijiji looking for people seeking a private PSW. I was surprised at the outpouring response. I created a schedule for myself with a few clients that had interviewed me.

I really loved working for myself. I loved the flexibility, I loved being able to schedule in my workouts and schedule time off for my mom without being told no, and I loved being in total control. In the back of my mind, I always wished I could have helped all those people who reached out on Kijiji but, only being one person, I was limited.

I was sitting in McDonald's one afternoon in October 2019 with a client of mine, and I was talking about the idea of opening up a private homecare company that serves all of the community I live in. We jokingly started writing down possible company names, not realizing one of those names would serve a purpose in the next month or so to come.

I went home and thought about the idea of opening up a company. The idea scared me. I had no business education; my background was in the healthcare field. I typed into the Google search bar 'Durham Region Small Business Help' and that is where I found our local business advisory centre (The BACD). I noticed they had a ton of free resources for people who were thinking about starting a company. I signed up for one of their information sessions which was followed by an additional three. The knowledge I had learned in just those four sessions was enough to light the entrepreneurial flame inside of me.

I was going to open a business.

In November 2019, my company Oakwood Home Healthcare was opened. Oakwood Home Healthcare was built on my experiences as a family caregiver, as well as my experience as a Personal Support Worker in the corporate world. Oakwood Home Healthcare believes in whole family care. Helping both our clients with the support they need at home, but also ensuring their loved one – the caregiver, is supported as well. I also believe in creating a good work environment for my Personal Support Workers – which is a profession that is often overlooked, used and abused.

My life experiences have led me to where I am today. Without the struggle, I wouldn't be anywhere near the Woman I am. The responsibility I took on at such a young age made me resilient. No matter how many times I get knocked down, I get back up. I can think back and remember often thinking "Why me?" *Why me?* You want to know why me? Because I was able to take the experience and create something beautiful out of it. The good times, the bad times, and sad times gave me the knowledge I needed to succeed. Every experience forced me to create a tool to cope with the situation at hand. Little did I know all these tools would later become something I like to refer to now as my caregiver toolbox.

My caregiver toolbox is full of resources. These tools include spiritual and self-care routines that I've developed into my schedule daily, weekly and monthly - I also refer to these as my "non-negotiables". It includes a list of what it looks like when I'm breaking down – so I'm aware of what that looks like – and as soon as I notice, I can take control and turn things around immediately. It includes my voice; because us caregivers are always going to have to advocate for our loved ones and lastly, the toolbox includes the care team for my mom, both her doctors and my family who have stepped in to help me. It includes the people I know that support me – especially when things get hard.

Just like me, you can do the same. One of the biggest lessons I learned was that even though I can't control what life throws at me, I can control how I react to it. Do I get upset with situations that are out of my control? Of course! But I'm also very conscious about how much energy I spend on those things – because chances are the longer I spend time wasting my energy on things that I can't change, the more exhausted and rundown I end up feeling in the end.

My recommendations for you going forward is to always take care of yourself first, especially if you are a caregiver. You cannot be your best self if you neglect your own needs. If you are experiencing any symptoms of burn-out, please contact your family doctor, or go to your local walk-in clinic. Do not wait like I did – because the longer you wait, the more debilitating it becomes. The hole you end up in, feels like you'll never escape.

Lastly, know this…*know that* you are strong enough and smart enough to achieve anything you want to in this lifetime. You are capable of fulfilling those big dreams you have for yourself, just stay focused, believe in yourself and be sure to create YOUR OWN toolbox for success.

MAKAELA MOORE

After spending many years gathering a wide variety of skills and a swag of qualifications, it was throughout the pandemic that Makaela felt like she finally came home. Home to writing. She has loved writing since her pre-teen years, always creating little stories and when she moved interstate in her early teens, she wrote letters longer than the lengthiest of essays to her good friend, who also went on to become a writer and successful poet later in life. In a world without internet, those letters were their lifeline, their connection, their confessional and they helped to develop Makaela's craft and passion for writing.

So after becoming a best-selling author for the first time in 2020, Makaela walked away from her 1:1 coaching and hypnosis business to focus on writing and getting back to her creative roots.

However, her love of personal development and brain science held strong and are now the main focus of everything she creates, including a range of books and digital products all designed to help those who feel like 'Hopeless Procrastinators' to achieve more out of their work and life by overcoming procrastination and perfectionism through self-mastery. Makaela says that when we become the fearless leader of our own life, our work becomes joyful, we become purposefully intentional and ultimately, unstoppable!

As a Certified Mindset Coach & Hypnotherapist with a Human Resources/Business Management background, Makaela thrives on sharing her knowledge of workplace relations, human behaviour, brain science and subconscious reprogramming with a good dose of intuition.

She's a multi-passionate entrepreneur, also owning a kitchen renovation business with her husband. She loves interior design, reading, writing, photography, acreage life and getting out with their caravan in tow, exploring all the beautiful places Australia has to offer.

Makaela's biggest pleasure in life is passing all this knowledge onto her most important creation and coaching client; her 9-year old daughter Sidney, whom she dedicates this chapter to.

Makaela Moore

Author, Coach, Hypnotherapist and
"Former Hopeless Procrastinator"
Brisbane, Australia

E:makaela@makaelamoore.com
IG: @makaela.moore

CONFESSIONS OF A HOPELESS PROCRASTINATOR

BY: MAKAELA MOORE

My childhood was spent in a constant state of daydreaming. Dreaming of a future that I honestly never thought was possible for me. I'd gaze up at the sky and imagine the big dream house with the white picket fence, the handsome husband in his business suit, and the 2.4 perfect children. As for any career, well, that never even entered my childhood stratosphere. Fancy jobs were only for smart people. I was not one of those people, hence why the daydream stopped at the letterbox on the picket fence.

Spending my childhood moving from state to state around Australia thanks to a military parent, I never fit in, never belonged anywhere. Homes were never 'home'; only ever a rented house in a patch of other army houses where neighbours were different from one week to the next. Everyone looked like gypsies in khaki. School kids like me, could never quite find their place before yet another uprooting and interstate move.

Life was a constant merry-go-round of packing boxes, new houses, new routines, new schools, but with the same old consistent fears and insecurities. They travelled with me everywhere I went, growing in strength with every year that passed.

I felt in this world, but not of this world. I was not welcome anywhere - a stranger in my own life. Not even feeling like I belonged in my own family. I was a pimple on the bum of life who didn't deserve a place at the table with the smart kids, the sporty kids or - heaven forbid - the popular kids. Nope, I relegated myself to a life of loneliness, boredom, books, art and daydreaming. I was welcome there.

Never living in the moment, instead always looking forward. To the next birthday, the next grade, the next stage of life, essentially wishing my life away. If I could just find some good friends, then I'd be happy. If I had some money to buy all the pretty things, then I'd be satisfied. If I had all the pretty things, then people might like me, and then I might have some friends. If only. If only I knew then what I know now, hey?

I was desperately seeking validation and approval - even just a whiff of being worthy or loveable became the unconscious theme of my life.

The first boy to pay me any attention at the tender age of seventeen had my hand in marriage at age 22. Within four years, my intuition was screaming at me to go discover life beyond a boring, oppressed marriage where self-discovery, personal development and further education were 'forbidden.' So I did. I packed my bags and left with only my clothes and pillow to start from scratch. It was worth every inch of pain, discomfort and difficulty.

Out in the world, actually on my own for the first time in my twenty-six years of life, was sink or swim. Except by that stage, I had dreams of a career that extended beyond any picket fence. And so began the hustle to create the life that I hadn't realised I'd been dreaming of since childhood. Fast forward through just over a decade of jobs, house-sharing, dating, world travels and becoming a university graduate (at age 35!), I was finally creating 'that life' and had a great job in a senior role.

But none of it was easy. I struggled every inch of the way. Every goal came with invisible chains, simultaneously holding me down and pulling me backwards. Never having been an achiever as a kid was etched into my subconscious. And so, pursuing a life of greatness, a life of reward and celebration seemed out of reach most days. Who the hell did I think I was trying to 'be', someone other than a pimple on the bum of life?

Oh, I can tell you who the hell I thought I was most days. A bloody imposter, that's who!

As a Senior Human Resources Advisor in a role advising several hundred people on workplace relations legislation and processes, with a university degree under my belt and at that stage a decade of industry experience, I did not feel worthy of holding such a position. Every day going to work, I was waiting to be told '*there had been a hiring mistake, but not to worry because they had a nice job on the front desk answering phones waiting for me'*. Of course, that never happened.

I had a memory like an elephant, could recite legislation off the top of my head and advise accordingly. I was incredibly efficient at that part of the job. It's obvious to me now, I was a valuable employee. But it didn't feel like it because I wasn't particularly good at managing my time, nor undertaking projects. Looking back, I can see I had the skills and knowledge to do the projects that I was tasked with, but there was always something stopping me - those self-sabotaging invisible chains. I was given projects to work on in addition to the parts of my job that I was actually really good at. In hindsight, it was the things that I was good at that kept me employed.

I'd start each day with good intention, the intention of being productive, of getting through the ever-ambitious to-do lists that I'd have created for myself. I prided myself on being someone who "bit off more than they could chew and just chewed really hard." And so the cycle would look very similar every day and every week. Start with good intention and often more than one to-do list, then progress throughout the day (or week) with roadblocks, U-turns and dead-ends at every turn. It was exhausting. I was working so hard, and most days were long days. Then I'd get to the end of each day and week, a complete wreck from working so hard that the only thing to do was pour a glass or five of wine afterwards. But, despite all that hard work, there wasn't a whole lot of productivity or progress happening.

I could see it, but I made excuses: constant interruptions, lack of resources or support, tech issues, illness. The excuses didn't actually matter. After a while, they were all the same shit, just wrapped differently. The constant "failings" were very obvious to me. I was terrible at my job and didn't deserve to be there. I kept being good at the parts of my job that were in my wheelhouse, to cover up the places where I felt I was lacking the skills, knowledge and experience. I did a great job of hiding my inadequacies. I was hopeless and I was the only one who knew it. My manager would ask how the projects were going, and thankfully, each time I'd made 'just' enough progress to be able to give him a glimpse of progress, but secretly, I was just dying inside. How long could I keep up the charade and keep this job?

There was one thing that I knew I was really, really, really good at. Procrastination. I was the fricken Queen of Procrastination. Look it up in the dictionary; there'll be a description along the lines of:

'Procrastination Queen' [proh-kras-t*uh*-**ney**-sh*uh*n-kween] *noun*: ~ woman who fluffs about all day, believing and projecting the perception of looking as if she is busy beyond belief, putting in long hours to substantiate and validate her place on the payroll, but ultimately achieves next to nothing and is worn out from dodging actual work all day long. Also known as a woman who feels overwhelmed and anxious thinking about all the tasks ahead, so finds coping mechanisms like food, alcohol, scrolling and oh look at that new bright shiny light over there…

And right next to that definition, will be a photo of me circa 2010. Smiling way too much, because someone once told me I had a great smile and now I believe it is my only good asset, so I'd better show it off in every damned photo there is of me (particularly if it's going in a dictionary for all to see).

I can see now that other people believed in me, my skills, my knowledge and my potential. But I didn't. How could I when I was never the smart or popular kid at school? I was just a no-one who slipped in and out of schools, flying under the radar of life throughout childhood, never realising any kind of potential. All I ever achieved or gained from childhood were a tonne of false and limiting beliefs.

I lied. There was that one time that I came third in a running race in the eighth grade. Only three people finished the race, but I was third … and of course, last! But I digress (I'm good at that! Oh look, squirrel!).

Looking back, procrastination and imposter syndrome have very much been the themes of my life in one form or another. I've always been a big dreamer; it was my childhood sport. I would dream, and I would read and write. I lived in a fantasy world in my mind that only I was privy to. Constantly making plans, lists, goals and lists of lists. I do love a good plan; it's like doing the thing without actually having to do the thing. Planning is the favourite activity of the Hopeless

Procrastinator because it's the vision, the dream, not the actual action. It is risk-free action, because you can't fail at something you haven't yet started, but, nor can you succeed, which is why I see the fear of failure and the fear of success going hand in hand.

When my daughter was five months old, I was in a period of trying to love motherhood as much as I loved my new precious bundle of joy, amongst all the reflux and sleepless nights. I was really looking forward to returning to my job in another few months to get some normality back. After all, at the age of forty, I was set in my ways and could see I wasn't cut out to be a full-time stay-at-home Mum. Redundancies were being handed out by the thousand at my department. Of course, one of those redundancies landed in my lap. I took it personally. They'd finally caught up to my procrastinating ways after all those years.

I then floundered for a few years finding my true place and purpose in this world. We combined my business knowledge with my husband's trade and started our kitchen renovation business. I learned a whole new world of skills and we were both 'all in' on this business, so it was sink or swim. We had to make it work, and work it did. I was tasked with all administration and customer-related tasks and he, the trade-related tasks. My brain coped very well with this work. With ten years of administration experience prior to my human resources career, this was so easy, I could do it in my sleep. I was managing a successful business and I was getting stuff done with the ease, efficiency and the consistency of the proverbial Swiss watch; it was all ticking along nicely.

Always the dreamer of bigger, brighter futures though, true to form, I found myself wanting more. More purpose, more passion. I was very comfortable, which had its advantages, like minimal signs of procrastination or imposter syndrome, but I was bored.

In hindsight I can see the perfect correlation between comfort and challenge, boredom and purpose, and of course, productivity and procrastination coupled with fluctuating confidence levels. It's like a perfectly choreographed dance of finely-balanced desires and limiting beliefs. Push and pull.

Consciously, I knew I wanted more. I still hadn't found my true purpose in life, beyond motherhood. To be frank, I can only articulate these feelings now in hindsight, with the wisdom and knowledge of someone who has spent the better part of the last five years doing deep inner work, discovering and uncovering subconscious beliefs and learning the inner workings of the mind.

I wanted to be more than the 'tradie's wife who did the books.' The reason I put myself through university in my early thirties was to be the person 'doing' the job, not the assistant. Looking back, I've always had ambition. After all, once a dreamer, always a dreamer. What I haven't always had is confidence or the awareness and understanding of the constant conscious versus subconscious battle in one's mind.

The pairing of my husband Graham and I is perfect. We're both big dreamers, but he has the massive advantage of being the original ADHD kid who can't sit still and when he eats that proverbial elephant, he takes several big bites at a time, always getting stuff done. He's the yin to my yang and the best accountability buddy I could ask for, always gently pushing me to get things done.

A classic trait of the Hopeless Procrastinator is not finishing what they started. Bright, shiny lights are very commonly chased like a moth honing in on a flame. New projects and ideas seem so much better and easier than the last. We seem to lose focus, not so ironically, right before we reach a peak. We give up when things get challenging, but more than that, we sabotage our efforts right before the breakthrough. Heaven forbid we allow ourselves to actually succeed!

Fear of success is a real thing. I remember the first time that concept ever occurred to me. I can't remember the situation, but I remember the revelation. I could see myself sabotaging my efforts and playing that awful game of conscious versus subconscious mind, where the subconscious in it's true stealth-like fashion, performs its job of keeping you safe just a little too well, leaving the conscious mind to pick up the pieces of a shattered dream.

The constant battle between the two minds is based in fear, uncertainty and doubt. It feeds off the distorted stories that we collect as children, not yet old enough to recognise or understand the complexities of life, therefore perceiving events through the filters of our limited experience.

So, why was I afraid of success? In my conscious mind, without a doubt, I wanted to be successful. I wanted to achieve all sorts of things, but what was waiting on the other side of success for me? The unknown was full of fear, uncertainty and doubt according to my subconscious. Consciously, I knew success would undoubtedly mean more work or more responsibility, and my subconscious chose to protect me from that. Only, I didn't identify it as that at the time.

The subconscious very cleverly disguised those fears as 'sudden disinterest' or 'change of mind' as the next bright, shiny light appeared on the horizon. But then, there are the days when it sneaks in and kicks you in the guts and unexpectedly presents itself as dread and anxiety, only you don't recognise it for what it is. You only know that life just doesn't feel good and you'd do anything for this horrible, dread-filled feeling to take a hike.

The subconscious also seeks pleasure and conserves energy. Both are very welcome traits of the procrastinator. We love the pleasure seeking side of the subconscious because humans will always choose pleasure over the pain of something hard, and as for conserving energy, well, we love our laziness too. Which is why most people have to push themselves to go out and do any form of exercise.

One particular project I was tasked with in my human resources role was developing an in-house training portal. I had the skills, knowledge and qualifications in human resources and training development to undertake the task. On paper, they chose the right person for the job, but reality didn't match the expectation. I took much longer than I should have to do the project. Some days I would literally stare at the screen, like an author with writer's block staring at a blank page. I knew what I had to do, yet my brain had completely opposing ideas. The invisible chains tightening around me, almost like I was being physically held back. Frozen in inaction. What if I finished the project? What would that mean? I can see in hindsight what I only intuitively knew back then. That the end of that project, the one that I was very comfortable working 'in', where I could indulge my rather strong penchant for laziness, would mean I'd then be given a new project to start on. Only, higher expectations would be placed on me, hence more responsibility and more work. My subconscious wasn't going to have any of that nonsense; protect and keep the human safe at all costs.

At seven years old, I learned a big life lesson. I was starting tap dancing lessons, I had my shiny black leather tap shoes and my pretty purple leotard, my short wavy hair probably hanging in my eyes, not pulled back into a beautiful tight bun like the other girls. I was ready for my new career as a tap dancer, except I was missing something. I had no metal taps underneath my black leather tap shoes, just regular bare soles. The metal taps were coming next pay day and I just had to wait. But I was the only girl without taps underneath my shoes and I was the odd one out. I was embarrassed we couldn't afford the taps and so, my feet barely left the floor the whole lesson to avoid anyone seeing my missing taps.

I just wanted to be like everyone else. I was already the odd kid out at school for two reasons. Having just moved to tropical North Queensland from chilly South Australia, not only was I the new kid in class, but everyone else could already swim. I wasn't used to the water, nor could I swim and was left to paddle all alone in the shallows while the rest of the class had their swimming lesson in the deep end.

When I got home from my one and only tap dancing lesson, I announced to my parents that I never wanted to go back. I quit! They never knew the real reason why I quit tap dancing; they never bothered to find out and they just let me quit. Several years ago, as I was trying to figure out why I wasn't finishing many of the things I started, the tap dancing story hit me like a freight train. I was allowed to quit then, so I believed I couldn't do hard things and quitting when things got uncomfortable was completely acceptable.

Therefore, my early years were lived completely inside my comfort zone, always taking the safe option, until the day I decided jumping out of a perfectly good aeroplane seemed like the thing to do. It was several months before I left my first husband and I was dragged along by my siblings. It was simultaneously terrifying and liberating. I don't know if it was the literal adrenaline shock to the system, the experience itself or a combination, but I was forever-changed that day. I could actually do hard things and I felt that if I could do that, then I could do anything. This is ultimately what gave me the courage to leave that first marriage and go out to chase my own dreams.

But even with that realisation, all those subconscious beliefs were still there, trying their best to hold me back and keep me living in struggle and hustle, which became a true love-hate relationship with myself and ultimately, self-sabotage.

When I did my coaching certification several years ago, I remember standing up in a room of approximately 100 other coaches in training. We'd been talking about coaching practices for different problems facing our potential clients. I was feeling extremely nervous to speak, but I asked our teacher about procrastination. I knew it was a problem, for me and many others, and I thought there'd be an easy solution for it. I thought he could tell me definitively that '*this*' was the why and '*this*' was the '*how to fix it*'. But he did not. In fact, his response had me perplexed. He said that procrastination was not an actual problem. He got interrupted at that stage and didn't follow up his answer and I left that room feeling confused, never actually getting clarification of his response.

I was confused, angry and determined to prove him wrong. Of course procrastination was a problem, otherwise I, and millions of other people, wouldn't experience it.

I set out to learn everything I could about procrastination, why we do it, when we do it, how we do it, who it affects and how to resolve it. Naturally, my first thoughts were of how to combat it through productivity hacks and strategies by joining that infamous 5 am club and collecting planners that ended up gathering dust. Those things all have their place and do work for some, but if the procrastination is as deeply rooted as mine was, then they'll only work for a day or a week; however long the willpower lasts. And willpower is a finite resource that needs replenishing.

I dug deep into the depths of my subconscious programming to discover why laziness had become my identity. Why I had become the woman who only finished things three-quarters of the way and then quit on most of them. Why I didn't follow through on things and why, despite all evidence to the contrary, I felt a complete lack of confidence to achieve and succeed. And even worse, I discovered a level of self-worth so low, that it's a wonder I've managed to achieve anything even remotely remarkable in my life.

A major turning point for me was hearing that everything in our life is a story. I wrestled with that concept, looking at it from all angles until it *finally* sank in.

Until we know the stories of our subconscious, we cannot begin to reprogram them. We tell ourselves stories about who we are and what our potential is or is not. Until we clear out the erroneous subconscious beliefs, we have no way of comprehending our true potential. Prior to that it's all just a far-fetched dream that we believe has no chance of manifesting into any kind of reality for us.

We allow procrastination and imposter syndrome to influence decisions, whether we realise it or not. Our subconscious keeps us in the safe zone. We don't push through that comfort zone because even though the discomfort is the key to our growth, it's just too damned uncomfortable and 'hard' in that moment. We give up short-term pain for comfort and therefore long-term gain becomes a life of mediocrity.

We can get caught in perfectionism, particularly when beginning a project. We procrastinate in moving forward and get stuck in reviewing, refining, redesigning, judging, changing and end up in a spiral of perfectionism and procrastination, which the more we do, the more we perpetuate.

Fear keeps us in pointless activity loops, cleverly disguising procrastination. Procrastination and perfectionism play into one another in an intricate way, ducking and weaving and disguising one another. But ultimately, disguising the true cause of it all, which lies beneath in the true depths of our self-worth.

Despite being born into this world perfect, whole and perfectly loveable, we humans lose sight of our value, our worth and our 'enoughness' through indoctrination. With each passing comment, interaction, reaction, communication or event in those early years, our opinions are formed and cemented into our very being and subsequently chip away at our sense of worth and value.

We crave attention, love, validation and acceptance. As youngsters, we are very creative when it comes to attracting the attention of our parents and others. As we grow, we attach our self-worth to external things like achievement, skills, knowledge, physical appearance, popularity, money and health. If we have these, then we are worthy, loveable and good enough. We feel complete. Or so we think, but do we really? If these things really did complete us, then personal development, coaching and therapy wouldn't be as lucrative or as popular as they are.

When we validate ourselves by attaching these external sources to our self-worth, it leaves us in a position of always protecting our position in relation to them. If we fail to meet the expectations set by ourselves or society, we intrinsically believe it renders us worthless. Our needs of acceptance and validation are not met and we can be caught in a spiral of avoiding the negative feelings, but instead feeling frustration at not having our needs met and we then buffer these feelings through distraction and/or self-medication via all the 'too much behaviours' like drinking, drugs and binge-eating. These make us feel better momentarily, but still leave us feeling frustrated that our initial need is still not being met, which can then lead to a depressive state, which is further exacerbated by the *comparisonitis-inducing* social media scroll.

When I look at my patterns throughout my life, particularly my procrastination, I can see that because my self-worth was tied up in all the external things, I was living in fear of failure. I was living and working from a place of fear that I wouldn't measure up to all the ridiculous standards I had created for myself through my subconscious stories.

All I could see was how much I wanted certain things in my life, whether career, finance or wellness goals. I planned them out meticulously, down to the smallest detail. Yet, when it came time to execute, I would always find some way or another of sabotaging my efforts. I literally felt like there were a set of invisible chains holding me back from executing my plans. I'd get the first few things done, but then habits would drop off, and excuses would creep in. The harder I tried, the more resistance I experienced. Why was I holding myself back from all the things I so dearly wanted in my life? The answer seems so obvious now in hindsight, but I was blind to it.

It took me a long time to figure out why I was sabotaging my efforts through procrastination and perfectionism. I was living in fear of failure, because failing meant I was not worthy, so instead of pursuing goals, I subconsciously sabotaged them to avoid any possibility of failure and therefore kept my self-worth intact.

One of the most crucial pieces to conscious transformation is identifying and then moving beyond those stories and limiting beliefs holding us back like those invisible chains.

Our subconscious programming is somewhat like the rings of a tree trunk depicting the age or history of the tree, with each year or event building upon and reinforcing the last, providing a perfect foundation for the next. Within hypnosis we regress through the years, back to before the very first event, before the time they ever felt the emotion that their limiting belief is attached to, in order to begin the reprogramming.

During this form of hypnosis, the hypnotist communicates directly with the subconscious mind, allowing the subconscious to be reprogrammed with a new appreciation, perspective and understanding of the situation or event and change the interpretations and stories like unworthiness, inadequacy and fear of rejection that were created from the initial event. Effectively, this rewrites history in the 'tree rings' of the subconscious and allows the person to move forward in life without the invisible chains of the old beliefs and stories holding them back.

The rings of the tree are very much like onion layers. Some of the most valuable lessons I've learned have been very surprising and even when I thought I'd reached a point of resolution or understanding, there was always another layer of the onion to peel back.

We find secret rewards in recognition, acknowledgement and attention gained from living by these rules and beliefs that we've been indoctrinated with and they have kept us stuck in a cycle that we just don't see. Like living in a cloud, unaware that a blue sky even exists beyond.

It's this very programming that holds us back from doing or achieving things we want. It is this very programming that creates the habits of procrastination, because it allows us to avoid the pitfalls of having our self-worth attached to external outcomes and situations, while not measuring up to unrealistic expectations we set for ourselves. So instead of making progress towards success, we hold ourselves back, remain stuck and ultimately fly under the radar, where our failures cannot be seen and therefore our self-worth is not threatened.

You can imagine how powerful it is to change the programming that is underpinned by all those limiting beliefs, getting uncomfortable, rewriting the beliefs and no longer fighting with your subconscious to make your dream come true. It is enormously powerful and while it can feel extremely hard, if not impossible in the moment, it is always possible and its incredibly rewarding on the other side. Regardless of the programming and beliefs that you've been brought up with, you can break free from them. In fact, everyone can because the ability to transform and create the breakthroughs are available to anyone who is willing to commit to and do the deep work.

Doing this work will be the reward of your lifetime and it is the reward of my lifetime to help others navigate this process.

MIKE COULAS

Dr. Mike Coulas is a Chiropractor who for more than 24 years has been caring for families and helping patients achieve transformational wellness results. Dr. Coulas is extremely passionate about chiropractic care and facilitating people to live an awakened life! He is a sought-after speaker, wellness coach, and guest on numerous radio shows, where he enjoys sharing ways to decrease stress on the body, mind, and spirit. Dr. Coulas has been a long-time resident of Whitby Ontario and continues to support the community as a trainer for various minor league sports teams. Dr. Mike Coulas holds a Doctor of Chiropractic from the Canadian Memorial Chiropractic College receiving both clinical and academic honours in 1997, and practices chiropractic, acupuncture and various form of energy work.

Learn more at https://awakenedlifechiropractic.com

HOW STRESS CAN WORK FOR YOU

BY: DR. MIKE COULAS

Stress is universal and something we all experience. I noticed something that causes traumatic stress in one person may have little stress for another. Our perceptions and how we deal with stress are unique to each of us.

When I was a teenager, I had what some may call a dramatic, stressful event.

From a young age, I have always strived to improve my health, wellness, and performance. In my early teenage years, to keep up and hang out with my older brother and his friends, I had to physically compete with them and have some level of success. To do this, I needed a certain level of strength, speed, coordination, and athletic abilities. These physical characteristics measured my health and success in fitting in and being accepted and valued by my older brother and his friends.

At this early stage in my life, I put my attention on my physical body. For many years I focused on being a better athlete. I played on many sports teams, and I competed and trained to improve physically, and the training paid off. I was awarded the male athlete of the year upon graduation from my elementary school. In high school, I became the captain of many successful sports teams that I played on, and we won many championships.

THE UNIVERSE'S PLAN ISN'T ALWAYS YOUR PLAN

When I was an eighteen-year-old high school athlete, I thought I had my life plan figured out. I was well on my way to excelling in university sports, and in my mind to becoming a professional athlete. Little did I know at that time, the universe had a much different plan for me.

When we were in the semi-finals of a major rugby tournament in my final year in high school, events unfolded that shifted my life path direction. It was a close game, and we were playing full out on the field. A full-back had the ball and was running hard to make a score, and I dove to tackle him, and that is the last thing I remembered before waking up in the hospital. I heard from my teammate Rob:

"Hey! Hey! He is coming to."

"Where am I?" I said groggily.

"You're in the hospital, Mike."

"What am I doing here?"

"You don't remember?"

"No!"

"You were knocked out!"

"How did that happen?"

"You don't remember?"

“No!”

“Wow, do you remember that big #20 guy on the Ottawa team?”

“No, I don’t remember anything.”

“Well, you dove and tackled him just before the goal line. You caught him, but his knee hit you hard in your jaw. It made a loud crack sound! We all thought he broke your jaw. He fell to the ground, and you just lay there. You have been unconscious ever since. That was about 45 minutes ago. How are you feeling?”

“A little foggy. I feel a strange electrical charge, like tingling going through my body. It feels weird.”

“Are you in any pain?”

“No, not really.”

“Well, you just took a pretty good blow to the head, Mike.”

“Yes, maybe I feel a little bit of a headache and a sore neck, but I just feel a bit woozy.”

“Well, I will get the doctor in here to give you a check over to make sure you're OK.”

Rob went to get the doctor, and I was just lying there trying to remember what happened or exactly who I was.

I did not remember the incident or that I was in a rugby tournament in Ottawa. I did not remember any of it, even though Rob told me that we were in our fourth game of the tournament. Memory loss had never happened to me before, so it was an odd and new experience. I don't know how much memory was erased, but I know big chunks of my human experiences were gone. I could not remember too much of that previous school year. I knew that all my experiences make up who I am, and the human conditioning and programming of these memories had been erased and altered. This experience changed my outlook on life, and it changed my personality. I knew that my personality created my reality, and my life path was about to change direction because of this event.

After the doctor's exam, I was released to my coach's care and my teammates with the standard concussion protocol.

Even though I was released from the hospital, something was not right in my body. My head was foggy. I had this constant tingling sensation stemming from my neck and going throughout my whole body. It felt like a mild electrical shock that didn't dissipate.

As time passed, I was losing weight which was unusual for me. In the first four weeks after the concussion, I lost 25 pounds. Something was not right, and none of my regular doctors had any suggestions. I was beginning to think the predominant tingling in the neck, back, and arms were something I was just going to have to live with. As I was sharing with a friend and teammate on the football team that I was feeling frustrated as I knew something was not right, he said:

"You should go get a chiropractic checkup to see if my chiropractor can help you."

"Chiropractor? Do you think he could help?" I asked.

He replied, "It's worth a try."

Knowing nothing about chiropractic, I agreed to see his chiropractor, Dr. Dave. After my health history, chiropractic spinal and neurological exam, it was determined I experienced the effects of an upper cervical spine subluxation. Of course, I didn't know what all of that meant exactly. However, he was particularly good at outlining it for me.

Dr. Dave explained the subluxation area I was experiencing could put pressure on my brain stem and could cause the tingling symptoms that I was feeling. He further explained that this area could lead to blocked energy in my body and could be the reason for the weight loss.

I felt relieved—finally, someone who could tell me why I was experiencing all these strange things in my body.

The blow to my head was the cause of the misaligned bones in my upper cervical spine. He proposed that a specific adjustment to the upper cervical vertebrae would be recommended. I was relieved at having someone who knew what was happening in my body and provided a treatment plan. I consented to receive my first set of chiropractic adjustments.

When he adjusted me for the first time, I heard, Crack, Pop! I instantly felt a change and said, "WOW! What a relief of pressure!"

It was amazing how a chiropractic adjustment could shift everything and make such a dramatic change. Right away, the tingling in my body was gone. I felt clearer and more awake. The brain fog was better, and I felt a sense of peace flow over me. It was an incredible experience.

I continued with a series of adjustments over the next few weeks, and I could feel the life energy coming back into my body. It was not long before I was back to my normal healthy weight. I was now starting to understand a poster that I saw in Dr. Dave's office. The poster was an expansive view of the clouds in the sky, and above the clouds, it said, "THE POWER THAT MADE THE BODY, HEALS THE BODY! IT HAPPENS NO OTHER WAY."

Dr. Dave explained that there is an innate intelligence within the body that flows from our brain through the spinal cord and branches out to all the body's living cells and tissues. Inborn, natural, innate intelligence is responsible for the development, adaptation, and regeneration of the human body. I was now aware of this amazing, intelligent energy flowing through my body.

AWAKENING FROM THE DREAM

One of the most profound things to come out of this experience was that I felt suddenly more alive. Like I had been in a fog or a dream before the concussion, and now I was completely awake. I did not know I was in that fog or dream until I was awakened. It was as though the blow to my head in that rugby game had to occur to have me go down the path to finding a chiropractor.

Before a seemingly random conversation with my teammate who suggested seeing his chiropractor, I had never really known anything about chiropractic or what they did.

Although my life focus up until that point of the concussion was on the physical, once having the blow to the head, it was almost like a literal wake-up call. From that point forward, I became more interested in exploring and developing my mental, emotional, and spiritual aspects of my health.

In high school, I continued to develop physically, but I also began to focus more on academics, and my mental knowledge and strength were improving. When it was time to graduate high school, I was offered many scholarships for both athletic abilities and academic abilities. I ended up accepting a full academic scholarship to York University in a program of kinesiology.

The most influential person to guide me to York University was the football team's head coach, who recruited me and let me know that my grades were good enough for the full academic scholarship and a few other benefits to going to York. He was also hoping that I would play for his football team. York did not have a particularly good football team. I didn't like the characters on the team, so I decided not to play. In hindsight, it allowed me to focus on my studies and allowed me to get good grades to get into a chiropractic college. Even in the early days after my first chiropractic adjustments, I knew that I would become a chiropractor. In my final few months of high school, I even did a class presentation on chiropractic. I felt I was destined to become a chiropractor. If he hadn't persuaded me to go to York and help me with the academic scholarship, I might not have had the same outcome.

STRESS CAN OPEN DOORS TO NEW POSSIBILITIES

A knee to the jaw is physical stress. Is that good or bad?

Most people would think that was bad stress. However, that knee to my jaw knocked me into a new life path—one I would not have chosen at that time based on my state of consciousness.

It was in my nature to attempt to tackle that player: after all, my nickname on the rugby team was "Killer Coulas." It just so happened his knee hit me hard in my jaw. I was knocked onto the perfect path to find the obvious benefits of the specific chiropractic adjustment. This, in turn, led to me learning about the art, the science, and the philosophy of chiropractic. Before this so-called trauma, I did not know much about chiropractic. I was interested in health, but I leaned towards becoming a professional athlete or gym teacher as a profession. I was smart enough to be a doctor, but something about being a medical doctor did not feel right. This natural healing approach of chiropractic made sense to me, and it felt like part of my life's purpose to become a healer instead of a perceived "killer" as my teammates had coined me to be.

The concussion that I received made me question the importance of the elite physical performance of the body. Now

I had a motivation to learn how to assist people suffering from blocked energy in their bodies.

When I started to study the art, science, and philosophy of chiropractic, I was mesmerized. It became my passion. I did everything I could to learn more about the profession of chiropractic. I visited other chiropractors; I called schools of chiropractic and looked at what would be required to get into these chiropractic schools.

I was so fascinated by chiropractic and how it had shifted things for me that it led me on a path of going to Chiropractic College and becoming a chiropractor. I explored energy medicine, acupuncture, and expanded consciousness. So, getting knocked unconscious by physical stress, a knee to the jaw, was a real blessing in disguise.

The study of chiropractic philosophy opened me up to the most important thing of my life, which became remembering my spiritual connection. It was important not only for me but also, I realized my connection and influence on everything around me. I now knew that I was a spiritual being having a human experience.

My physical human part seemed only to be the visible "tip of the iceberg," while the spiritual side had been unknown to me, like the big part of the iceberg hidden under the water.

After the blow to my head, I started to contemplate some of these life questions:

- What is our life purpose?
- Why are we here?

- Do we live a thriving life, or are we just trying to survive?
- Are we looking for things that can be threatening in our environment, or are we enjoying the never-ending changes presented to us?

I am a big believer that there is a reason for everything, and that one event set me on a different path than the one I had planned for myself, including opening up to looking more at the spiritual connection to all things.

MAKE STRESS WORK FOR YOU

Stress is constantly influencing you. You can't avoid it; you can't hide from it, in life things happen, one after the other. When things are happening, it's throwing your brain and body out of balance. The body has a fantastic ability to know what to do to bring this balance back to homeostasis. Some stressors are obvious, and some stressors are subtle. Some stress is beneficial, and some can be harmful, especially if it becomes chronic. All living organisms can adapt to short-term stressors, but the chronic ones can lead to a state of dis-ease and eventually to pathological diseases.

There are three main types of stress:

1) **Physical** – like sports injury from trauma.
2) **Chemical** – like toxins in your food and environment.

3) **Mental/Emotional** – like the death of a family member.

Our bodies have an amazing ability to adapt to all kinds of stressors.

Physical

If I regularly lifted heavy weights, certain muscles would get stronger. If I practice shooting lots of basketball free throws, I will become a better shooter. One stress, physically lifting heavy objects, can make you physically stronger. The other would build your mental/emotional confidence so that you can perform this activity with a high level of success. Then if presented with having to shoot a game-winning free throw, you would have had lots of experience shooting these shots, and you know you could do it. So, you may associate fun with it. But if you have not practiced that shot much, you may get nervous, especially in a game-winning or losing situation. That mental pressure can cause you to perform poorly. This poor performance will make it likely that your muscles will tense up and lead to a missed shot, and experience emotional trauma from the reaction of your peers.

Chemical

We are affected by stress in many ways, and some of them will be obvious, like in my case, a knee to the jaw, which was a physical trauma that knocked me out cold. We also have subtle stresses that are happening all the time. For example:

- Chemical toxins in the air we breathe or the food we eat.
- The thoughts we are thinking.

Chemicals in our air, water, and food may seem more obvious however thoughts are a huge contributor to most people's trauma.

Mental/Emotional

Most people are overly critical of themselves and have negative self-talk going on throughout their day. Often your inner dialogue will be thoughts of worry or fear. All these thoughts are making things change in our body and throwing us out of homeostasis. Your thoughts can create a wide variety of chemical and hormonal changes in your body to adapt to the stressor and your meaning that you equate to that stressor.

We can live a Pronoia life instead of a life of Paranoia.

According to Wikipedia, pronoia is the opposite of paranoia.

- **Paranoia** - A person suffering from paranoia feels that persons or entities are conspiring against them.
- **Pronoia** - A person experiencing pronoia feels that the world around them conspires to do them good.

I like the title of Rob Brezsny's book; *Pronoia is the Antidote for Paranoia; The Whole World is Conspiring to Shower You with Blessings*. I believe this to be true, and we have a choice.

If you are living in paranoia, the reptilian part of your brain is thinking about the worst-case scenarios and how we can fight, flight, or hide. If we see life as hostile, we are always looking for danger around the corner. We are not in the present moment. We are thinking about survival and self-preservation. We are thinking of the future, or we are thinking of what happened in the past. This is a stressful way to live, and it can have a profound effect on the health of our body.

We are all in a constant state of stress, and our amazing body is always adapting and moving back and forth towards achieving some sort of balance. Some stresses are greater, and more obvious than others.

Living on planet earth there is always gravity acting on us along with all other kinds of environmental stressors. We are constantly adapting to these stressors of the environment that we are intimately connected to, and we unconsciously accommodate them. A more obvious or greater stressor would be like getting into a car accident or a knee to the head. These types of stressors will initiate a more conscious and noticeable adjustment. For every action there will be a reaction whether we are aware of it or not. It is beneficial to know that we are not separate from our environment, and we are constantly attracting a variety of stressors based on our frequency of thoughts, feelings, and actions. As Albert Einstein said,

> *"The most important decision we make is whether we believe we live in a friendly or hostile universe."*

Our perception of reality, what is happening, and the meaning we put on it, can determine how we react or respond to it. When I envision a reality of love and abundance, I feel safe, secure, and satisfied. I know that everything is connected and working in harmony. This way of thinking, feeling, and acting takes practice since my original conditioning had been one of seeing everything in my reality as separate and finite.

THOUGHTS ARE THINGS

I believe that thoughts are things. Anything that has been created in this world started as a thought first. We create our reality based on our thoughts, feelings, and actions. Our feelings create a body frequency that attracts similar frequency things into your life. Often thoughts of our past will hold a frequency of guilt or shame. While thoughts of our future may create a feeling of fear or lack. I have learned that if I can be here in the *now* moment that there are no problems. Living in the present moment is the goal.

In my exploration, I found several questions that helped form the reality I wanted to create. Do I want to live in paranoia or pronoia? These are questions you too may find of benefit and can contemplate and journal about:

PARANOIA	OR	PRONOIA
Are there conditions outside of me against me?	OR	Are things happening for me?
Do I have to be on a high alert for survival?	OR	Can I go with the flow?
Do I live in fear?	OR	Can I live in the love of whatever arises?
Am I a finite, separate, fragile being who needs to be in fight or flight for my survival?	OR	Am I an infinite creator of my reality?
Do I live in a limited reality of lack?	OR	Do I live in an abundant reality?
Why do I feel depressed?	OR	Can I choose to be happy?
Can I forgive that childhood trauma that is causing me to feel depressed?	OR	Are my challenges there to help me grow and to become who I am today?

How we envision our environment can determine how our body reacts and determine the life we will create based on our meaning of these thoughts.

CHRONIC STRESS

Many people in today's society are living in a state of chronic stress. They don't know how to take a break from thinking stressful thoughts. Even if they are in a situation that most people think is safe, they are still looking for potential dangers. This creates body chemistry that throws us out of balance.

Most acute stress is manageable, and it is normal to experience it from time to time.

Our bodies' autonomic nervous system has two modes:

1) **Parasympathetic** – This mode is our rest and digest mode that allows us to regenerate. This is called the parasympathetic part of our autonomic nervous system.
2) **Sympathetic** - The other mode is the sympathetic nervous system. In a stressful survival situation, we produce chemicals that allows the body to fight, flight, or freeze and hide.

The body can only be in one mode or the other. When the body shifts from one mode to the other it is accompanied by thousands of body chemistry changes.

If we live in the sympathetic nervous system too long, we will create a body that will start breaking down. It will get to a state of Dis-ease. If we stay in this state of Dis-ease too long, it will start developing abnormal body tissues, which can lead to pathological situations and serious diseases.

I often see patients coming into my office who experienced that final straw that "broke the camel's back". This may present in acute back pain or could lead to something mysterious like an autoimmune disease.

If we can bring the body back into the parasympathetic mode for longer periods, our bodies will be able to regenerate and restore our natural, well-being, state of health.

8 TECHNIQUES TO HELP WITH STRESS

Some of my favorite tools to help bring the body back into the parasympathetic mode are:

1. **Meditation** – There are many types of meditation that you can explore to find what resonates best for you.
2. **Yoga** – There are various types of yoga, and all have the mind-body connection to help in destressing.
3. **Grounding or Earthing in Nature** – You can explore using a Grounding Mat or simply go barefoot in nature or walk barefoot on the grass.
4. **Breathwork** – You can explore the breathing techniques of the Wim Hof method or Soma breathing by Niraj Naik.
5. **Energy Healing** –My favorites are Reconnective Healing or Complete Cellular Mind Body Alignment.

6. **Acupuncture** –Traditional Chinese Medicine Acupuncture and Acupressure have been used for over 2000 years.
7. **Chiropractic** – I am trained in many techniques, and I prefer Hands-on Diversified adjustments.
8. **Massage** – There are many types of massage, and I prefer Deep Tissue Massages.
9. **Heart Coherence Training** – Heart Math Inner Balance device gives you Biofeedback of your Heart Rate Variability.
10. **Emotional Freedom Technique** – Also called Tapping, is a great method that combines tapping acupuncture points with powerful affirmations.

LIVE AN AWAKENED LIFE

I believe that we all came here to have a human experience. When we are born into this world, we soon begin to get programmed to what our parents, our society, and culture think is important for our survival and what is perceived as important to fit in. As a result of this programming, we have amnesia to who we really are.

Often this conditioning leads us to perceive many events in a way that perpetuates us to experience personal suffering. All the stresses and suffering that we go through are the catalyst for us to wake up and remember how connected we really are and to awaken to a more conscious life.

Our experiences have been perfect to create who we are today. We need to learn how to love who we are and forgive all of our challenging experiences that brought us to this perfect present moment.

My mantra is *I want to live an Awakened Life!* Every day I wake up and realize that I am a spiritual being having a human experience. My awareness of this has transformed my consciousness.

When I woke up in a hospital with amnesia, that memory loss allowed me to release from my story. Since that day, I see the world in a whole new light. It is perfectly imperfect. I can choose to be happy, and I believe that I live in a friendly universe. I have learned to slow down and breathe into my heart, get out of my head and stop thinking and judging so much. Now I find ways to have joy in my life journey. The key insights I have gleaned from that experience that may be of value to you are:

- Life is a soul adventure.
- Our purpose here is to wake up!
- Remember how powerful you are.
- I trust that everything is always working out for my highest good.
- I have transformed my consciousness so that suffering is optional.
- I can change my beliefs to help empower my human life adventure.
- Live an Awakened Life!

A few additional things I remind myself of every day:

- Follow your passion.
- Act on your excitement to the best of your ability.
- Be aware of your thoughts.
- What you put your attention on is where your energy goes.

We are the architects of our own lives. There are no mistakes, and it is never done. We are always learning and making choices. We have free will to make more loving choices. When we wake up to the realization that we are all connected, and at some level, we all come from one creative source, then we will be more compassionate to others. We will learn to truly forgive others and ourselves. And remembering everything that is reflecting back to me is exactly what I need to learn at this moment.

Be here NOW!

As Eckhart Tolle said,

> *"Stress is caused by being "here" but wanting to be "there"."*

This NOW is our present moment, and we can choose to appreciate whatever comes next.

Living a more awakened life is my focus. I feel my life's purpose is to help others wake up from the dream and live an awakened life. Together we can make this world a better place.

I invite you to live an Awakened Life!

PART 3

AWAKENING

FRANCES ADAMSON

Hi, I'm Frances Adamson, and my gift and purpose in life is to create the conditions to experience happiness, calm, and ease, in my body and heart. A big part of finding this ease and steadiness comes from teaching and sharing what I've learned over my life.

I was lucky to be encouraged creatively as a child, to start learning yoga at a young age, and to have active time outdoors; the three pillars of happiness.

Still, if like me, you share this goal to be at ease, you can see that life, being imperfect, has dealt us blows, and unless you were born enlightened, we must work your way up out of the mud like the lotus to bloom.

Exploring yoga, art, and intuition over many years, guided by compassionate and experienced teachers, has led me to a deeper understanding of how using the breath and body tunes us into our heart so we can heal and thrive.

Breathing mindfully is at the heart of yoga, and available to anyone who wants to learn it. Finding blocks and releasing them can become as effortless as pausing in life for a few minutes to observe and shift your breath.

That's why I created Joy Core Connection and my yoga programs. To share the knowledge I've gained over the years, and help you find the best ways to reach your goals for living with ease in body and mind.

Everyone is unique and practicing yoga can and should be done with ease, whether you can touch your toes or not. Finding where you are at the present moment in body and heart is a creative process, one that is supported by a practice designed for comfort and enjoyment.

When I'm not having fun helping students open their body and mind, I'm a wife and mother; cooking, gardening, and making art.

LEARNING TO BREATHE

BY: FRANCES ADAMSON

My mother's eyes were amber gold with brown flecks, her favourite song was "Hard-Headed Woman", and most people would remember her smile, which was wide, and her laugh, which could escalate to no-holds-barred shrieks of delight.

She got angry with just as much passion though, and then her eyes started to swirl deep inside like the Tasmanian devil's in *Bugs Bunny*. Seriously, and the child responsible for that shift was usually me. I never saw how much alike we were because of that held-in quality she had after the divorce.

My father was tall, dark and handsome, a romantic idealist. His vision of my mother as the perfect woman was shattered on their honeymoon. He had borrowed a convertible to drive his bride home in, but got lost in the backroads of rural Alberta.

She knew the area, but he refused to just let her drive, and after a heated argument, she insisted he pull over and went running off into the field screaming. Day one and the power struggle was on.

Although my parents really tried to be amicable when they divorced, my mother's anger was never far from the surface. I didn't know the reason, and it took years to process once I learned it and to understand the guilt she would have felt at what happened.

By the time mom was pregnant with me, the marriage was toxic. There was a fight, he punched her and broke a rib. It must have been misery for my mom, the physical pain of a broken rib while carrying me, a constant reminder of the emotional pain of her failing marriage, loneliness and isolation.

The child in the womb, flooded with stress hormones, must be affected- the 'fight or flight' system triggered. Perhaps this is why I was a 'sticky' child. Mom said she lost the other kids at the mall, but never me. Like the umbilical cord never was cut.

We were four kids, 9, 7 (me), 5 and 3. Raising the *mob* was not much fun for mom after dad left. I was the designated shit disturber, and I heedlessly expressed all the pent-up rage and frustration for the family. Although my mother was unhappy in her marriage, this was 1970, and she had no family close by and had been too busy to make friends.

Besides the swirling in my mother's eyes, her whole face contorted with rage at times. I had no idea what she was going through emotionally. I was seven, and I was torn apart by my father's leaving too. Looking into that well of darkness, I made an assumption that I caused this reaction; I was flawed.

With a nervous system set on high alert and an internal belief that I was unworthy, I was highly reactive to how everyone around me was feeling. I was sensitive to being judged or criticized, and the underlying anxiety drew teasing and abuse. The problems in the family got worse, and by the time I was a teen, I'd been kicked out of my mom's several times, and then kicked out of my dad's. I moved out at 15.

Mom died last year, and I knew, undoubtedly, that she loved and respected me, and I loved her too. Worming that secret out of her was good for her, and I finally found out what was 'wrong' with me.

She lived in another province, so I didn't get to say goodbye. Actually, I was working. I was preparing a yoga course to launch online. I was working because I thought: *How will I be able to finish this in mourning? If I can just finish it before she dies, then everything will be ok, I can launch when I'm ready, I won't have lost momentum on this months-long project; I will be a success.*

It wasn't far below the surface, though, an ocean of feeling: I am nothing, this class is nothing, I never really proved to my mom I was worthy; if I can just finish this, even though she is struggling for her last breath at this moment, she will know, she will know.

I got the call though, before I was done.

It was much worse than I imagined; I was numb and unmotivated. The best way to describe it was that I was becalmed on the ocean, suddenly, after fighting a gale all my life and using all the rage and its force to drive me forward. It was gone. I was adrift.

Even though my mom and I had healed those old wounds in so many ways, they still were working away inside me. I made them part of me. They were, and still are, complicating my way forward. At the same time, they have driven me, motivating me to dig deeper into where I am now, who I am, what I truly want.

It is a continuous process, and new layers are always revealing themselves.

Consciously transforming - what is it? All our lives, we grow and change. To consciously change is to choose the direction and actively work towards it.

There is groundwork for this process, and that is self-observation.

It's not enough to know what transformation you want. Without taking the time to understand clearly where you are, and who you are at present, your efforts to change won't progress. When I first started practicing yoga, the idea of self-observation made me cringe.

I felt and sensed that I was defective in some way, both in my physical being and personality. Was I a 'people pleaser'? Absolutely. In a convoluted way. If I was unworthy, which I believed, then efforts to please others could not possibly succeed. Although I tried.

Thus it was I lived in a paradox that created a fault through my being. I tried to please people but harboured a deep anger at the impossibility of it. This was not a good recipe for healthy relationships.

I was so incredibly lucky though! In many ways I was unconsciously transforming through yoga. *Consciously* I studied every way I could to understand my personality so I could fix it. It was an impossible task. We cannot change certain things about ourselves.

When we try, people sense it. They react with the very opposite of what we hope for, especially if you are a transparent type. Even though they may not figure out what it is, they sense the flaw, the vulnerability, the need. We never get respect and appreciation as an 'imposter.'

In my experience, it's not possible to please other people. After many long years of frustration, I just brought down more and more judgement. Finally, I realized that pleasing myself, including both my human body and my heart's desire, is the most pleasing thing I can do for *everyone*.

And the more I tune into it, the more I am ok with being imperfect or being rejected or judged by those I love or anyone.

I have a large, outgoing personality, and I have 'samskaras'—ingrained patterns of behavior—I react before thinking.

The study and analysis of my personality was useful in that I became educated enough to know that I wasn't alone in my difficulty, and that there were many positive aspects to my makeup.

It couldn't reach the true cause of my suffering though, because it didn't change the patterns ingrained in my emotional makeup and my body. We can see and understand that our personalities are complex and wonderful, and still keep reacting as though we know we are unworthy.

Things really started to happen for me though, the more layers I peeled off in this self-observation exercise called yoga.

I first discovered yoga in a recorder class at the age of seven, right around the time of the divorce. My teacher had long brown hair and wore earth tones, this was 1970, and she taught us yoga in order to settle us down. Then we learned to play the recorder— tunes I could still play for you to this day.

Afterwards, I would walk home in the dark, Winnipeg after 5 pm, frosty and clear, the snow crunching as I walked. I sang nonsense songs out loud as I went, until I reached the back lane. There I would stop for a few moments to hug the telephone poles which hummed with life.

I was tuning into a deep sense of peace and relaxation within myself, and a feeling of connection with a larger energetic field. I took my time approaching home with its noise and strife that would erase the mood. Even though I would not regain that feeling with such depth for many years, I knew it was possible, and I never stopped looking.

When I look back now at my own marriage, it was just as doomed as my mom's. I left Manitoba for B.C. after a failed relationship, and after gallivanting about as a gypsy dancer and a palm reader. I was 37 and alone.... lonely, despairing that I would ever find love.

I met my next partner at a nude beach in Vancouver, and one thing led not just to another, but two kids. We moved to Toronto where I started a yoga studio, but things went more or less the same as my parents' relationship had gone- toxic.

It was during this time that I learned about some breathing techniques that saved me. In a workshop for yoga teachers on Yoga Therapy I was in such bad shape, that at one point I was lying on the floor silently crying because I couldn't do a headstand without a wall for support.

The teacher, Mark Whitwell, was talking about the four breathing techniques used in Yoga Therapy. These are: the pause, ujjai breath, an even breath, and a smooth breath- all for the purpose of lengthening and slowing down our breathing. He also brought up the point that yoga is a practice. That we learn yoga so we can practice it daily, to feel better.

I found a teacher in Toronto who was from this same lineage. She taught me that self-observation was not done with the mind, by reading or studying or anything like that. It was way simpler: just pay attention to the breath.

The trouble with relying on our thoughts to transform us (i.e. positive thinking, affirmations, goals, intentions, etc.) is that we as humans are complex and live with paradox all the time. Therefore, we can hold within us the thought 'I am worthy' and trigger the old neural pathway 'I am unworthy' simultaneously.

Through yoga, we seek to bypass the thinking mind, the prefrontal cortex. Instead, we invite that part of the brain to have a well-earned break, training it to hold a single focus while we let the body and unconscious have a chance to express themselves. Observe the breath, observe yourself.

'Following the Breath' is a very fundamental method of communication between all the intricate and numerous processes that make up our whole being. It's the method of finding out where we are. Instead of mental analysis of our thoughts, it's taking the time to experience your energetic/physical state on a subtle level.

The breath tells us when we are calm, the movement of our chest with the breath reveals tension in our shoulders which shows us our stress level. We can tune into clues almost like an outside observer. Is the breath smooth or are there little catches and stops; is it fast or slow, shallow, or deep? These tell-tale signs do not lie and we can train our mind to observe them.

We train to observe our breath to know where we are *inside.*

When I feel triggered, I can focus on relaxing and sensing ease and release in this area. I get out in nature and I self-soothe; I work on new patterns of behaviour. I also accept it, work with it.

As we observe, the body naturally changes. The breath slows and becomes smoother and even. If we consciously take this further, finding ways to keep our breath slow, rhythmic and regular, we enhance this effect. From knowing *where we are* in this moment, we can move in the direction of where we want to be.

Relaxed, calm, aware of our emotions being triggered, able to self-soothe and enhance feelings of well-being—this is the goal.

For me, the pain I feel when I am triggered into hopeless rage—the feeling that I am unacceptable as a human being—manifests as a knot just below my solar plexus. This is a source of power. We want energy to flow through us, not knot up inside our muscles and tissues.

My daily practice sets the stage for this. It trains the mind and body to reach that pleasant physiological state of whole-being wellness; I am connected to that feeling as a refuge.

When I fled my toxic marriage, back home to Winnipeg, these skills helped me survive. Far from being a refuge, I walked right into the lion's den with my two boys. Old family patterns that had been dormant for years were awakened. No one wanted me to remind them of past trauma, and I was shunned.

My mom helped me, and my dad would have if he hadn't been prevented. The rest of my family subjected me to all the old judgement and abuse, no one could see me as I was, or how much I needed their support. I was shut out, so I moved back to Toronto, on the assumption that my ex-husband at least had the support of his family there.

At the time of my mom's death, I had come a long way. I was happy and feeling balanced in a long-term relationship. My boys were loved by us both, and we were settled in a nice house in a nice town.

On the other hand, I was so used to struggling with rebellion and people-pleasing, I still hadn't teased out that knot of low self-esteem. And now, the force that was my mother was gone and I felt like I was out on a wide ocean with absolutely no idea who or where I was. I really reached an inner block.

I so identified with being an inwardly-thwarted artist. My yoga career was both rebellion (it's not an easy career) and an attempt to find acceptance. I had trained and trained to be highly qualified, and launched into yoga therapy—a widely unknown modern evolution of yoga.

Shortly after mom died, a friend of mine in real estate happened to phone me the week before I flew out to my mom's celebration of life, "Did you want to sell your home?"

It so happened I did. I had been feeling we had outgrown our house, but hadn't spoken it out loud yet. It was incredibly surprising when my husband agreed to let me put it up for sale and so, in the three days before our flight I sprang into action, got a handyman to fix a few things, repainted the trim a fresh white, and put as much stuff as I could into storage.

From being becalmed, I felt a strong and steady force fill my sails with purpose, I was in action. I felt tapped into what I truly wanted. Our family needed space. I needed to be closer to nature, regardless of what people thought, I was going for it, and now.

We got an offer while away at my mom's celebration of life, and a boondoggle over the possession date meant we ended up homeless for a month, staying with different relatives. Although it was stressful, there was a sense of having stepped into a vortex where things were happening that would carry us forward if we didn't fight it.

I was chastised from all sides. But for the first time in my life, I trusted myself. I knew that I deserved to be happy, to have a house that would fit us all and my business.

I was a little on edge as we muddled through the move three months after the death of my mother. As we drove to pick up another load from storage, I was suddenly overcome with painful thoughts of my father.

My husband pulled over because I was sobbing uncontrollably. "It wasn't his fault, it wasn't his fault," I said through the tears. I clung to my husband for all my life. My feelings took me back to the time that I flew back to Winnipeg and found that my family would rather shut me out than be reminded of the past trauma.

I wept because I knew that in my heart I had been blaming my dad too, and it hurt so much. In that moment I released it, I realized my dad would have helped me if he could, that he was too elderly to fight or even understand. At the time though, I was very hurt that he let things happen the way they did.

Now, twelve years later, I sobbed into my husband's chest. I said, "He didn't know what was happening, he didn't know. He wouldn't have let it happen if he knew". I can't really express the depth of feelings about what went down all that time ago, when I fled home and found out it wasn't the safe place I had always believed it to be, that it never had been.

When I calmed down, I phoned his nursing home but got the answering machine. He was pretty far gone at 93, but I could tell him how much I loved him. I called my brother, "Please get him to call me."

My brother called that evening. Dad had died a couple hours after I called him.

I have been assimilating the belief that on some level, my dad was the only person who ever truly loved me, and he was gone. A false belief, surely. A complex and difficult knot.

The move has proved completely beneficial. We are now near a ravine with a beautiful creek where I walk almost daily. There is no traffic noise; it's quiet and lovely, a sunny spot facing south which I love. We have enough room to have big dinner parties and to each have our own space, and for me to have a comfortable office, art studio and yoga studio.

It was a year before I resumed my project to build my online course- 'the Joy Core Connection 12 week yoga program'- to help others build the foundation to ease in body, mind and heart, like I did. Only instead of taking years to figure it out by trial and error, I want to teach all the best and most effective tools in a matter of months.

No sooner did I get started, when the first lockdown of the 2019 pandemic happened. During that year, I focused on me and family— taking a break from teaching and time to really figure out what I wanted. I also see that what I have learned in my life so far is badly needed by so many people who are hurting.

It's been a long slow unwinding. In yoga we say we never really change the 'samskaras'- or underlying patterns. We only cover them over. It's like when a tree grows on the side of a cliff, twisted, but strong. Even if the wind stops blowing, and the rain finds a hollow to water it there, the tree will be what it is.

I'm ok with that. I have covered over that pain, but I know where to find it. It's a beautiful scar. A scar to remind me who I am, where I am.

Today I am more fully committed to sharing what I learned than ever before. Instead of coming from a place of proving myself, that I am worthy, that I have value, I come from the deep desire to help other people heal the way I healed.

Finding Refuge in a Greater Truth

It was in the spring last year, at the beach, just me and my little white and orange terrier. The sun was shining, the waves crashing on the shore in a stiff southwest wind. My head's down, hood up, absorbed because I woke with the thought that something special will happen today. Will an old friend call me up? Will I find a treasure on the beach, or maybe I'll be inspired to write a song…?

I look back on the difficult year, two deaths, and a move. A lot of processing life and grief consumed my energy and time.

No conclusions that satisfy me, as I proceed, head down, scuffing the sand and rocks beneath my boots. Heaven, life after death? I have a sense of each spirit opening like a portal into this world, like an eye blinking in the fabric of the universe, outside of time and space. I sense that my mother and father are a part of me, and that their presence has rippled out through the world, becoming a part of everything- eternally.

Suddenly, a wave crashes right in front of me intensifying the luminous colours of the stones beneath it, sparkling with light flashes and glitters. Not water, stones, and light; but a joyous burst of intelligent *life*- a presence, a message- that was my dad!

I feel eternity, the connectedness of all things, and the impossibility of death. Everything is ALIVE; I yell out to my dog Chloe. She obviously agrees, looking up from some bits of rotten stuff on the beach with joy.

Together we continue our walk, my heart at ease, re-connected to that truth that I learned so long ago as a child; observing the body and breath, the secret to tuning into the wisdom of your heart to heal your wounds.

JO MAZGAY

Jo Mazgay founded West Coast Soul in 2016 as a line of positive affirmation women's t-shirts. Little did she know then the power of positive words.

Since 2016, West Coast Soul has umbrella'd multiple heart led ventures, classes and programs such as Goddess Flow Yoga, retreats, classes in Women's Empowerment, Women's Sensuality and a youth program, to name a few.

Jo grew up on the West Coast of Canada in a beautiful small town, and has carried the positive impact of many of the people she knew there forward with her in life. She currently runs her Women's membership program Soul Journey virtually, as well as her youth program, Generation

Empowered virtually, but will be back in studio as well post-Covid.

Jo has been asked to teach for associations like Big Brothers Big Sisters, and is often asked to speak as a guest expert in events for women's programs.

As a single mom to 4 kids living in Simcoe County, it is her real life experiences that will catch your attention, but her quick wit that will capture your heart. She tells stories that relate to women of all genres, with the raw and honest ability to laugh at herself. She has an authentic ability to showcase vulnerability and courage hand in hand. Jo's accomplishments in life, personally and professionally, are all inspired by her drive to lead by example. Showing not just her own children, but youth from her programs, and women who need to see it to believe it, that it does not matter where you start in life, you choose the ending.

This life is yours to live on your terms.

Jo can be reached via her website WestCoastSoul16.ca or WestCoastSoul16@gmail.com to explore more programs, stories and upcoming events or book for speaking engagements.

AUTHENTICALLY ME

BY: JO MAZGAY

I am a spiritual entrepreneur.

I advocate for women, children, and all other vulnerable sectors in society.

I run women's circles, empowerment workshops, retreats, kids groups, youth camps and more.

When you google 'types of entrepreneurs', spiritual rarely pops up. Social, maybe. So you might ask: what is a spiritual entrepreneur? And I just might tell you that I am quite certain I am making it up as I go. Just as there is no blueprint for a former red-neck, trailer park girl like me, who grew up in a small logging town to become spiritual, there is absolutely no blueprint for what I do in my career.

I follow my gut every single day. That's my biggest constant.

My gut, my heart, my soul lead every decision I make. I have not always been so free to do so. Along the way, 'pivot' has become my catch phrase.

Here is what I do know to be true. To be a spiritual entrepreneur, to have the courage to stand in your truth every day and 'sell it', it is crucial that you are also connected to your authentic self. You cannot do this work without authenticity. You cannot "fake it till you make it". Your truths, your passion, your ideas, and what you stand for are what attracts your like-hearted clients to you.

Before we launch into that though, let me ask you this:

> What is it that is driving you forward? What is it about being an entrepreneur that is enticing you?
>
> Spiritual or not?
>
> Can you own it?
>
> Have you had a personal experience that has transformed or inspired you?
>
> What is your story? Do you feel confident standing in it? Does the world need to hear it?
>
> What have you learned that was not taught in school?
>
> Have you ever seen a product, service or recipe come up and thought "I could have done that", and feel like you missed an opportunity?
>
> Do you constantly challenge norms and think outside the box?

If you are smiling because those answers came easily to you, then you my friend, just might have what you need to be a spiritual entrepreneur.

I'm not going to lie to you and say it is easy, but when everything aligns, it really is much easier. First, however, you must come to a place of confidence in your own spiritual connection. Be conscious of who you are, who you are not, and why you want to be here. Are you willing to do the shadow work?

What is your story, what brought you here, to this place that leads you to want to do the work? Every single one of us has a story that will bring you to tears. A story that will motivate you, validate you, and inspire you to be the greatest version of you. Some of us will take a transformational experience and build a new life from it. One that serves others while also giving our own lives purpose.

This my friend, is just the condensed version of my story.

When I was young, I never fit in. I didn't think like other people. I lived in a tough town and I thought I could change the world by just being kind to it. Fairy tale thoughts I know, but I had it in my mind that there was so much more for me out there. I could do more in life than what my local high school counselors had presumed. Growing up in the back of a trailer park, their sole goal was to get me out of high school before getting pregnant. There were no college pep talks or applications offered to us.

Toxic masculinity ruled the 80's. Homophobia ran rampant. Extreme indulgences were common place. The more you showed off, the more successful you were. Did you ever watch 'Married with Children'? The blatant egotistical ignorance was celebrated.

Women wore shoulder pads to feel like powerful allies within a male-dominated business industry.

We were programmed to believe the masochistic fear that other women are our competition, at school, at work, and in relationships. Ladies, we must stop blaming the other women for husbands, boyfriends and partners who cannot stay within the perimeters of the relationships they committed to. We were programmed to never rock the boat. Children should be seen and not heard, do not stand out and most important of all, never ever bring shame to yourself or your family.

And yet, I never believed it. I looked for the good everywhere, I had so many questions: why was life not fair? I always cheered on and befriended the underdogs and the vulnerable. I led with kindness, and as much as the world threw adversities at me, I still tried. I tried until the world kicked my ass.

For a short time, I fell into a toxic relationship.

All I am ready to share about that situation is: that someone telling you that you are nothing over and over again and asking you what is wrong with you has a profound effect. The damage of feeling alone, isolated, scared and different, and the grief of everything you thought you knew in the world being stripped away from you, is a lesson in human survival like no other.

Leaving this relationship, I had to start again and heal deep generational wounds alongside my own with no idea who I was, what way was up, or how the fuck I was going to survive.

There are triggers, so many triggers, but also a will to not just survive, but to thrive despite all I had been reprogrammed to believe I was (and was not). Rock bottom desperation hit me at age 25. I knew I had more in me then what everyone who knew me gave me credit for. But I also had such a fear of rejection, judgement, and failure that I did not know how to stand in my own self with confidence. I knew deep down, that I had the ability to change or influence this world. I could and would thrive and change the world. I just had to figure out how. I began by essentially mimicking those I saw as successful, on how to survive, to succeed, and to make ends meet.

From the outside, it really looked like I was doing well. By mimicking, I was beginning to change my mindset of how I wanted to move forward, who I wanted to be and what was going to be my legacy? I was employed in a thriving company, working my way up one day at a time. Whatever they needed from me, I did. I educated myself by reading and researching everything I could. I took every course, weekend and evening trainings, shadowed those who had climbed the ladder themselves and took their leads. I studied successful women, I listened to their stories, held space and grew. I saw the difference glaring at me every day, between my bosses' lifestyles and mine. But I also knew, I had what it took to be more. I just had to learn the ropes first. I learned, I absorbed and I mimicked, everything I could from this job, so I could apply it to my own when the time was right. It was only just the surface though, I still had real work to do inside.

I worked hard, got married and had children. We had a dog, a beautiful home, everything I dreamed of as a child; things I had been reprogrammed to believe that girls like me, never got. Everything I 'should' have to make for a happy life.

Yet, I was still unhappy. The more my husband tried, the sadder I was on the inside. The lonelier I felt. Surrounded by people, I felt completely alone. Unseen. Fraudulent. The more material gains we acquired, the more disconnected I became.

I tried going back to work, for someone else.

I tried working from home.

I tried a new career.

I would wander through the self-help sections of book stores seeking a cure for my loneliness, but nothing matched what I was feeling.

Then, late in my 30's, I remember, being hidden in the bathroom, door locked, shower running, crying at my reflection. I was looking in my mirror, but I had no idea who I was.

Who was this woman I had become? Whose life was I living? Where did my passions, my dreams, my purpose go? Then, like a shot, it hit me. I wasn't living true to me. There was nothing in my life that was authentic to me. It was all for show.

I was living that life of "should".

I should have a house with a white picket fence, a nice car, a perfect exterior. I should raise perfect children in a perfect suburb surrounded by other perfect families. We should have holidays on beaches and birthday parties with Pinterest themes and invite people who were good for career and social growth. Not my children's friends. The one time I went against all that, held a princess party for my daughter, invited her friends, the social blow back was swift and painful. I should be happy all the time, because my husband worked so hard to provide me with this lifestyle. And he did, I still appreciate that.

I wanted to throw up the "shoulds", because none of them were aligned with what I wanted. My girlfriends wanted to lay on the beach of an all-inclusive retreat, drinking margaritas all day. There is nothing wrong with that, there really isn't. However, I wanted to go and help at third world country orphanages. Experience different cultures, taste their foods, see the country past the swim up bar.

I craved a life of meaning. I wanted to build the shed, not make it pretty. I hate housework. I needed to create community that was like-hearted to me, yet I was so immersed in my husband's world, because it checked all the boxes of how I should be happy. I felt if he was good enough, then by being married, staying in his shadow, perhaps by default I might be too. Maybe no one would notice what a fraud I was. Living a life of lies, all for show because I thought that would make me happy. This was causing huge strains on my marriage. The more he tried, the worse I was. Until finally he left. Divorced at 40. *Motherfucking pivot.*

Here my friends, is the biggest lesson I have learned in life, so grab your highlighters. Personally, professionally, where ever you choose to show up, if you are not showing up authentically, you will not be happy. You will get called out, you will not be successful. That is an absolute fact.

After the summer of my 40th birthday I had huge personal shifts. I was fighting suburbia every single day to live my life my way. My marriage was gone, I was now a single mom to four kids, and I had not worked a "job" since before my third child was born. I had a great little hand-made jewelry company going, but with no time off parenting to run it, I had to close it down to be the full-time parent my kids needed me to be. I had to figure out, who the hell I was, and how I was going to move forward. Suburban gossip ran rampant. I quickly learned who my friends and supporters were and were not, and that's ok. If I am honest, how can I have been 'heart-fully' connected to anyone if I was living a life of appearances? It was time to take my life back, and live it my way. Authentic to me.

Life lesson number 371 from that summer: sometimes, your friends, colleagues, family even, do not want you to change. Even for the better. Me changing, growing, and shifting, made a lot of other people uncomfortable. What I learned is that it can make other people evaluate where they are at, and if they have settled. "It's good enough for me". "Why can't you just be happy?" I heard these a lot. No one wants to admit they settled. We are all doing our best to get through this life. Some of us choose to showcase only their highlight reels on social media, giving an image of perfect lives from the outside. I just could not do that anymore. My growth also made me less likely to be a willing doormat to some agendas, so relationships evaporated fast. I have my own thoughts on this, but that'll be the next book.

Becoming spiritually conscious, is a life-changing experience, and, it's not often pretty. Even a caterpillar turns to 'goo' before growing wings. Whether the trials themselves transform you, or you experience revolutionary growth, wherein you not just survive then begin to thrive, your life changes.

The most profound lesson I learned throughout all this was through a small group of women, who showed up, day after day and just held space. They had no agenda. Spread no gossip. They did not bask in the glory of my falling. They did not choose sides or point fingers. They reached out their hands, held my head above water and showed me community. They fed my children, they fed me, painted my walls and helped me prep my marital home for sale. These women brought food, took my kids out, wiped my tears and worked tirelessly to show me I still had self-worth. I always had it, a failed marriage didn't take that. Little did they know, this was just the beginning of me finally finding self-worth.

Whether they knew it or not, these women had given me illuminating revelations that would change the trajectory of my life. So much so, that my new life mission became to create a community of supportive like-hearted women. Women supporting women. I had never experienced this to this extent. To release the programming of mistrusting other women, create a safe space for women to come into and learn, explore, and feel who they are. To understand that within The Divine Feminine, we all rise up together, in support of one another. All of this went against everything I had ever been taught, shown, or experienced. But my goddess, it felt good. This needed to be shared, the story of women holding up other women.

My next lesson? How? I'm not a coach (yet), a psychologist or a therapist. I was a single mom with no idea, just a vision. I simply had a longing for a community of support, kindness, laughter and sisterhood.

There's no blueprint for that either, so I hope you are comfortable *pivoting* (side note, huge growth comes in the most uncomfortable times).

The sweet truth is, that living your own life authentically, manifests the next steps over and over again. Imagine walking along the yellow brick road, and the bricks only appear beneath your feet if you trust enough to step. Trusting. One brick at a time to appear. That's how this felt.

I also did one big jump within all this. I moved. I left the small town where everyone knew who they thought I was, and moved my family to a new city. A city where I could simply start living my life authentically, with less preconceived judgements. This was good and bad. It was great because no one looked at me like I needed to be committed when I put my crystals on my windowsills, walked in the dirt barefoot, 'saged' my home, danced in the kitchen singing to my kids into a wooden spoon, while syncing my calendar with the cycles of the moon. However, building a business in a city where you know two people, can also be a bit of a challenge.

I had to build community, a like-hearted community. And this might be an interesting time to note, I am an introvert with social anxiety. Fun times right?

One of the most healing tools I had when I was still fragile post-divorce was Goddess Flow Yoga, a very feminine and sensual yoga developed by my friend. It was freeing, it was fluid, and it was a back to the nature of being a sensual woman without shame. I loved it. Week after week, women came together. Young, old, petite, curvy, some with life lessons to share. Some, like me, arrived completely broken. I learned to not just hold space, but to be vulnerable enough to allow myself to be seen. Be seen broken and vulnerable, and allow women to hold space for me. I searched high and low in my new city for something similar, and when I found nothing, coincidentally (if you believe in this word) my friend reached out as she was offering a Teacher Training for her Goddess Flow Yoga. Intuitive nudge, intuitive push, intuitive hit-me-over-the-head-with-a-brick, opportunity. I registered and spent six months travelling back and forth for the 200 hour training I needed to become a certified teacher and booked a class. I was so excited to share all I had learned this far. Share my healing with women who had felt as low as I had.

Guess what? Crickets…

Build it and they will come is bullshit.

I put my class out on FB, Instagram, Twitter, invited my two friends and my neighbors. Nope. It was too new and uncomfortable for some to be so expressive. No one had heard of it. Also, I learned, even though I had done my self-work; that did not mean anyone else was ready to do theirs.

I had to learn how to be an entrepreneur in a way that was authentic to me, teach my way, and keep going against the grain. I have lived my whole life like a salmon, always swimming against the current. I was used to that. I was not deterred now. I had felt the magic of The Divine Feminine connection. I had to find a way to work for myself that still allowed me to raise my kids hands-on and keep growing, I had so much growing to do and needed stay connected to me. I really loved this me I was finding.

What I learned was this.

Spiritual Entrepreneurs are driven by a desire to serve and uplift others while also bringing themselves joy. The joy is in the work. This is work I would do (and have done) for free because it is so self-fulfilling. You will never live a fulfilled life disconnected from your own values so, creating a career that is aligned with your values feels like magic. Do not let others tell you who you are, find you and put you out there. Your truths, your stories, your offerings that are aligned with your soul, will attract back like-hearted clients. There are billions of people on this planet, enough clients for everyone in every business. Authentic business relationships come from building and nurturing the relationships. Relationships are attracted to you by commonalities in personal, energetic, and professional lifestyles. Like-hearted and like-minded attractions are magnetic.

You will inspire others by having the courage to be vulnerable, and they will follow you to see if you stay aligned. This is human nature. As humans, we are social creatures who thrive on being connected. Entrepreneurial ventures start from a place of passion. Whether you are a social entrepreneur, spiritual entrepreneur, small brick and mortar business, you made the conscious choice to create your own niche, with your own passion, so be bold!

Do not be afraid of failure. Failure is a lesson. A lesson is an opportunity to pivot, shift, grow and move forward. In life, personally and professionally, we have choices in how we move forward from any lesson presented to us. Grow from them, then take those lessons and inspire others.

When I found the courage to put my authentic ridiculous self out there, without worrying about what others would think; only then did I find that I attracted the most incredible clients and friends a girl could ask for. By having the courage to take off my societally accepted mask, I let them see me. I was accepted as I was, in all my glorious weirdness. I could be myself, and that felt good.

In the past five years, I have grown my Goddess Flow yoga practice into Friday night events consisting of a Woman's

Circle experience. I created a circle within an atmosphere of a safe and sacred space, giving them an experience from my heart. Next came empowerment workshops, and a youth program blossomed. Then came an investment in studio space, a boutique, and regular classes filling up. I finally felt my life was mine for the creating. We even put a float in the city's Santa parade.

Then, Covid hit and the world shut down. *Pivot.* How do we create this virtually? Creative thinking. We opened it up to women from further away, right across Canada. Week after week women from across Canada, from the US, and from New Zealand showed up virtually for our Soul Circles. Next, the studio I had invested in had to close. Pivot. Now I must find a way take my experience further. Pivot. We began having the youth program virtually, mini virtual retreats. I was staying aligned to my goal, staying connected to my why, still inspired by my transformation. If I had let the ego gremlins in my head get stuck on the loss of the physical space, the shame of perceived failure, I wouldn't have experienced the growth of women from across Canada now joining us weekly.

Because I stayed focused on my desire of providing transformational experiences to women, I opened my mind, got creative and stayed in my truth.

No matter what gremlins or lessons the world throws at you, remember why you started, and that you are absolutely worthy of not just having desires, goals and dreams, but also of reaching them. Jim Rohn says, "If you really want something, you will find a way. If you don't, you will find an excuse." It would have been easy for me settle into self-pity the summer my life transitioned. I could have let the anger, grief and rejection bury me and settle for a job that just paid the bills, but I chose instead to take a chance on myself, believing that I could gain so much from this alliance of women. Imagine how much healing we could bring into the world by paying it forward, and making a meaningful career out of it.

And on a final note, although likely the most important advice I could ever offer anyone professionally or personally, listen to your intuition. Do not allow fear or discomfort to hold you back. There is no timeline, no too late for living your dreams. Every experience you have had in this lifetime has in some way prepared you to rise into your genius. On a planet of nearly eight billion people, there will be many who are 5, 10, 20 steps behind where you are now and in need of your advice, offerings, or products. When one person has the courage to step into their vulnerability, by sharing their story, their wares, and their ideas, it gives others the courage to find their courage as well. If you are not chasing your dreams, whose dreams are you chasing?

What is your dream? How does it feel when you imagine it? There are no dreams too big to imagine. If you can imagine it, you can create it. Sit down, close your eyes, and picture yourself in one year, five years, seven years, living the life of your dreams. How does it feel, how does it taste, smell, who is with you? Intuitively does it make you feel excited? Your intuition, that gut feeling, butterflies, they are there to guide you. Your head will fill you full of gremlins, all the things that could go wrong. But your gut, your heart and soul will always intuitively show you what can go right.

SARAH STERNBERG

Sarah is passionately committed to helping women shift from traditional roles in society to becoming whoever they want. With radical self-acceptance and responsibility, women move from feeling quiet, hidden, and trapped by success to becoming unleashed, vulnerable, real, and empowered. That's where women see true success.

Sarah helps women gain freedom, confidence, and abundance. When women accept themselves unapologetically, anything becomes possible. Their opportunities open up.

Songa Designs was born in 2011 out of healing that followed one of the darkest moments of her life: her mom's suicide 10 years prior. Graduating with an MBA in 2008 when the world wasn't hiring, she found herself on a deeper search for meaning when she agreed to volunteer as a business trainer for women's cooperatives for two weeks in Rwanda. Over two decades later she is still intimately involved with the country and the business she started with some of the artisans she trained.

Sarah continues to collaborate with female creators in Rwanda who are all business owners, artists, and visionaries. By cultivating financial independence and self-love, she supports women in their growth to become leaders who share and uplift the voices and expertise of other women around the world.

You can reach Sarah at sarah@songadesigns.com or visit SongaDesigns.com to view the artisan's handcrafted designs.

FINDING FREEDOM IN RWANDA

BY: SARAH STERNBERG

Let's talk about boobs. It always amazes me how much of a public debate erupts when a woman in the United States breastfeeds in public. When I was working with all-women cooperatives in Rwanda, breastfeeding was commonplace. Kids were crawling everywhere. Diapers were being changed while I was teaching the mamas how to calculate profit margins on their handmade crafts. And boobs were being whipped out when it was feeding time. It didn't even cross my mind that this was a big deal.

Finding myself walking the red dirt roads framed with enormous banana trees in Rwanda's rural provinces was a total fluke. The last decade of my life had been in the predictable 9 to 5 grind, never questioning going outside the traditional narrative of working for a living. While the recession of 2008 devastated the income of many Americans, it was my window to escape the life I felt expected to live. Freshly armed with a useless MBA, I jumped on a 35-hour journey to the other side of the world. It was my opportunity to leave all expectations behind, volunteering in a country I had only recently located on the world map.

One of my friends said she had a contact in Rwanda who was looking for a volunteer to teach soccer to elementary school kids. Since I used to play soccer in my high school years and it's a sport I love, I thought I had a strong enough resume to qualify. In fact, twenty-five years later, my dislocated shoulder still plagues me. It was not the best reminder of my days on the field, but good enough to land me the position!

Two weeks after landing in Rwanda, I was feeling lonely and at my wits end. I'd scheduled appointments with the head of the soccer non-profit, and she was either a no-show or ended up canceling on me. I had to accept that this soccer volunteer gig was a mirage. It didn't exist, but my perseverance did. It was as if a part of me already knew that my time in East Africa, in the specific country of Rwanda, was no coincidence. If I took a magnifying glass and inspected within myself, I'd discover there were layers that felt safer hidden. Rwanda would eventually expose the heavy sadness that I had buried for so long.

I went through a range of emotions, from feeling bummed that I was so isolated and lonely, to mad because it took a lot of effort to be there, and I wanted to make this experience one that I'd remember for a lifetime. The uncertainty and empty days fueled my thoughts that I was on the verge of deep depression. There were a couple of mornings where I woke up and thought, "Gosh, I could lay here all day." I never did—I always dragged myself out of bed. Then one morning, I finally got sick of my pity party. I just woke up and said I needed to snap out of it! I needed to *make things happen* instead of waiting for something to happen. So I sent out a series of emails to local contacts I found after researching on the internet.

I also took advantage of my time without any responsibilities. I discovered live singing at Hotel des Milles Collines (a symbolic hotel made famous by the movie *Hotel Rwanda*), met a Congolese man who spoke French and taught salsa, and became friends with the manager of a local coffee shop in Kigali and helped him write a business plan. I was just discovering how much this country was going to change me forever.

When I first met Amara, she showed up with her blonde hair pulled back into a tight ponytail and she had a notebook and pen in hand. I knew immediately she was a straight shooter and didn't have time for anyone's crap. Being direct and to the point, were characteristics I noticed from others who were long-term ex-pats. She was an overworked and underpaid non-profit director, and I was hired to help relieve some of her duties. I remember Amara's signature ponytail and whip-smart business sense. While all the interns said she was a tough boss, I knew she'd do pretty much anything to help them progress in their careers.

She was running multiple departments with up to ten interns at any given time. The organization's mission was to educate women's cooperatives with business lessons while connecting them to a global marketplace. After sitting in on some of their training, I learned that the interns were all Rwandan and part of the Orphans of Rwanda organization. They all happened to be young men in their early twenties, and their school was paid for by Orphans of Rwanda. They were hired to run the training in the cooperatives and provided valuable input into the curriculum while incorporating feedback from the artisans.

I fell in love with the interns! They each had their distinct personality and were like most young people – they wanted nice cars, cool clothes, and to impress the ladies. What I loved the most was their everlasting respect for the women. And the feeling was mutual. The cooperatives treated the interns like they were their own sons. Seeing their mutual admiration underscored my strongly held belief that involving local people in a non-locally based organization should be a requirement! It goes without question that Rwandans are the most qualified to truly understand their own culture. Placing locals in positions of power also holds them accountable and empowers them to be directly involved in improving their surrounding communities. Also, it broke down the dehumanizing and disempowering stereotype that only "mzungus" (foreign people) can save them.

After earning respect from the intern team by showing them I knew a thing or two about business, Amara eventually gave me free rein. However, she emphasized that she needed a lot of help with supervising the training sessions, which meant monitoring the interns and making sure they were doing their jobs. I had a choice between working with the computer skills or the business plan training programs. I chose the latter.

Walking to my first cooperative, I navigated a rocky and uneven red dirt path narrowly outlined by two high brick walls. Anyone could have easily missed the turn down the alleyway that led to the seamstresses without very detailed directions. As I entered the small, aqua blue room, I saw many brightly-colored fabric pieces printed with intricate designs, blanket the hard cement ground. Later I'd learn this was called "kitenge fabric" or African wax print fabric. I could hear some foot pedal sewing machines operating fervently by the seamstresses, and the dimly lit room had one small window which opened up to the next building's brick wall. There were beautiful sewn designs hung all over the walls and three rows of sewing machines with four women working on them simultaneously. Maybe two of the women glanced up at me and the other two just continued with their work. Let's just say I was unimpressive to the artisans.

"Muraho!" Pronounced mer-rah-hoe and means "Hello!" was my first attempt at greeting them in Kinyarwanda, their local language. It was met with laughs, but it warmed them up to me. The Bantu language is filled with more consonants than vowels making it difficult for me to pronounce correctly. Too much emphasis on the wrong consonants was the difference between saying "chair" versus "fart." However, I learned quickly that each woman started their name with the title "Mama," which was then followed by their firstborn's name. I met Mama Merci, Mama Tito, Mama Christa, and so many more. It was beautiful to see their identity wrapped up with love for their children.

Little did I know that stepping foot into the small seamstress cooperative was only the beginning of an amazing and lifelong transformational journey. Of course, you never know that you're going through something transformative when you're going through it. Instead, I just took in the sights and sounds of this beautiful new country. It was so green and so lush with banana leaves blanketing the endless hilly mountainsides. The miles of red dirt roads always led to a new and incredible experience, and the hours spent in the artisan's cooperatives were good for the soul. The close connections I made with some of the mamas slowly influenced me to open up deeper and reflect on the tragic loss of my own mom.

"Sarah, you raised me!" It had been almost a year since I started working with the women, and I joined Mama Carene, one of the leaders in her seamstress cooperative, on her long walk back to her home high on top of the countryside. Mama Carene was as thin as a yellow No. 2 Bic pencil, with a smile that could light up any dark night. As thin as she was, she had already birthed four children! Her home was perched on top of a steep hill, and if you ever got caught driving on this hill during a rainstorm, be prepared to get stuck. It happened to me once, and I had to flag down four friendly Samaritans to lift my car out of the ditch I slid into when the tires gave in to the slick, muddy road. Once you made it to the top, there was an immediate sense of community. One walk down the main road with my arm hooked with Mama Carene's arm, and I had instant street cred.

Mama Carene's cooperative was the first one I stepped foot in. The seamstresses were beyond talented and could make anything you asked them to. They didn't even need a pattern. After working with them for a couple of months as their business teacher, we talked about our language barrier. It was like I was attached at the hip to my translator, Jadot, because without him, there was very little chance I'd be able to communicate with the artisans.

Jadot is one of those people whom you meet, and you can't imagine life without them. He had the most infectious laugh, always a sparkle in his eye. He understood the "way of the mzungu", and so he was always invited to all the important international donor meetings. He immediately connected with anyone, both visitors and the artisans. He had this way about him that was understanding yet firm, and could explain concepts to the women in ways none of the interns could.

While I struggled with learning their language, some artisans expressed interest in learning English outside of the classroom. I made a general offer to all the artisans to sponsor their education if they wanted to continue learning English. While many were excited by this prospect, only a couple approached me, but only one stayed dedicated: Mama Carene. Classes cost less than $3, and I also paid for her moto rides home at night. This was one thing she also requested since it would take her two hours to walk home, preventing her from regularly attending classes.

I knew Mama Carene was destined to chart her future on her terms. The stories I picked up from the other women were that her husband spent more time in bars than at home helping raise their four boys. She was now motivated to earn her own money. For two years, Mama Carene consistently showed up to English classes. The organization I worked with noticed her eventual fluency in English and soon hired her to be part of their team! Within three years, she had her first trip to the United States. I am so proud of her. Now the world is her oyster!

When she credited me for "raising" her, my first reaction was to deflect the praise. But as we were walking to her house that night, it struck me how one small action can completely change the trajectory of a life. I learned that many women are saving money for school fees and the basic necessities of living, like food and rent, so a small investment in learning to speak English was a luxury few could afford. Mama Carene saw a future self that her sister seamstresses could not see in themselves, and she went for it!

About an hour from Mama Carene's seamstress cooperative was a group of thirty artisans who are expert basket weavers. It was mesmerizing to watch their weaving process.

Mama Dan explained, “Sisal plants naturally grow in our backyards among the banana trees. The fibers in the sisal leaves are used to make the baskets.” She then demonstrated how it works: they take this solid long sisal leaf and place it between a hard rock and a sharp knife. I watched her pull the leaf between the knife and rock; the solid leaf was transformed into thin, natural-colored hair-like strands. These strands were then dyed to the exact colors specified for baskets.

The other weavers shared that they designate a day to dye the newly created sisal fibers in a big meadow in front of their cooperative. Each woman would come with enormous bushels of natural sisal. One woman was in charge of boiling the water with the exact measurement of dye they needed for whatever color they wanted the natural sisal to look like. The process of dyeing all of the natural sisal would take all day, and then the freshly dyed bushels had to dry in the cooperative overnight. Once dried, the artisans would craft these gorgeous baskets with the most intricate patterns and the brightest colors.

I came to know this weaving cooperative the best.

“Hey, sis, are you busy?” Jadot called and asked me. It was a Saturday, and we normally took the weekends off. He said we needed to go out to the countryside to visit the weavers. When we arrived, it was just Mama Kenny sitting alone in the cooperative on the floor on a straw mat of her own. She had a bright red wrap on her head and her usual African mama attire:

a long piece of kitenge fabric around her waist matching her blue shirt. Her youngest, four-month-old Energie, was crawling on her outstretched legs, completely unaware of her mom's tears. Mama Kenny rarely spoke, but she had this powerful presence about her.

She requested our visit because she just needed someone to talk to. Her husband was abusive and last night was another traumatic episode after he came home from work. There were plenty of other women in her cooperative who had lovely and supportive husbands. Unfortunately, Mama Kenny was not one of them.

She has always been one of the more quiet women in the cooperative. So I was astonished when her usual soft-spoken self, started opening up about her life at home. This woman who was always so reticent was pouring out her soul, and I wanted nothing more than to find a way to protect her from her raging husband.

"There is nothing you can do. I will leave him when the kids are older," she said.

She wasn't asking for anything more than just to have someone listen to her. Just listen. I started to understand that, at least in Rwandan society, a woman's self-worth is so intimately tied to that of how many children she has and her marital status that she tends to lose her own identity. It is worse to be judged as a single mother of four children, than to endure daily beatings from your husband.

I knew she came to like me because she renamed Energie "Baby Sarah." This was done jokingly since I had no kids. To not have kids as a young woman was not widely accepted in Rwandan culture, so she named one of hers after me. As I listened to Mama Kenny's story shared with me through Jadot's compassionate translation, I understood that she needed a possible escape plan from the abuse and would I be able to help her. I felt a certain closeness to her. We couldn't speak the same language, but I was honored that she felt she could confide in me. We left with her knowing I would do anything she needed to support her.

As I drove home, I thought to myself: am I crossing the line of being a teacher/mentor versus being a friend to the artisans? I wanted to remain professional, but it has always been my natural instinct to be a friend before anything else.

Ten days after our surprise weekend visit, Jadot received a call from Mama Kenny's husband. "The shit left. Mama Kenny is such a bad person."

On the same day, we had scheduled training at her cooperative. Some of the other members were there but not all of them yet. Around the corner, Mama Kenny appeared with a bunch of bags. She threw them in the back of my seat, and she sat in the front passenger seat with Energie strapped to her back.

"Her husband locked her and the baby out of the house all night last night," Jadot said to me. I drove off with Mama Kenny and Energie without asking any more questions. Jadot stayed to do the training. I pushed away the feelings of lines being crossed from professional into personal and I was not going to kick her out of my car.

Mama Kenny stayed at my house in the city for two weeks. We kept her location secret from other members, mainly for safety reasons because I wasn't sure if her husband was looking for her. My western-style home with hot running water and electricity did not seem to faze her. She had no interest in my full kitchen or bathtub with a shower. Sometimes I'd look for her, and I'd find her in the back bathing her baby in a small bucket and pouring warm water over her. A few weeks later, she returned home when her husband found work in a different province in Rwanda.

Spending so much time outside of the classroom with the women was such an enriching part of this experience. They let me "in" to their world. They invited me to many morning teas, dinners and weddings. They constantly questioned when I'd find a husband again and prayed I'd have a child eventually. I felt like a member of this amazing extended family of strong mamas who thrived on the love of tradition and connection.

It raised this question within me: was the love by so many mamas my path to healing after losing my own?

I remember the day so clearly, even though it happened over ten years earlier. I'd gotten home from work and was still in my knee-length red skirt, white shirt and just pulled my hair up into a ponytail. I looked out my window, and the day was still unusually sunny for San Francisco. My dad's name lit up my caller ID, and I immediately answered. His first words were: "Are you sitting down?" It was then he shared the devastating and tragic news that my mom had taken her own life.

If there were ever a time I felt my legs immediately transformed into heavy cement blocks, this was the moment.

"The police are here to remove her body," my dad said as I sank into my chair after my knees gave out. I would have never imagined that I'd lose my mother at the young age of 26. It was the darkest moment of my life.

"Your mother loved you so much," his voice said as he was trying to get through the tears.

My dad decided to hold a memorial service a year after her suicide because the shock and sadness were so heavy. My beautiful mom had battled mental illness for as long as I could remember. It was on that unusually sunny, summer day when she decided she no longer wanted to live in pain. On a boat in the Gulf of Mexico, my family gathered together and shared our memories of my sweet mom. Her ashes scattered on the water; that was the last time I remember thinking about her untimely death. I thought if I erased it from memory, maybe it wouldn't be so painful.

Unresolved pain has a way of leading people down the road less traveled. I knew that I wouldn't have unconsciously chosen to be in Rwanda for so long if there wasn't something unhealed within me. It never crossed my mind that the healing power of 150 strong and wise Rwandan mamas is what would change me forever.

I didn’t quite appreciate the women's strength until I learned more about the genocide that tore their country apart in 1994. It would be extremely ignorant and disrespectful to visit Rwanda and not understand its history and how it still deeply affected the survivors who still live with the violent memories to this day.

I wanted to educate myself about the genocide, so I decided to visit the memorial sites on my own. After hearing my Rwandan friends share some of their survivor stories, I knew the sites might be so gruesome that my rational mind didn’t want to believe what happened.

On a cloudy day, I jumped on the back of a random motorbike, and my driver’s name was Charles. I became fast friends with Charles. He was a skinny driver and patient with my limited Kinyarwanda. It was a slow Saturday, and I think he was just happy to earn some money. He took me to a Catholic church where over 6,000 people died. This site was chosen because his cousin, Francois, was a tour guide there.

Francois led me to the top of a below-ground memorial on the outside of the church. I was told that it held coffins and human remains. I almost didn’t go down there. I peered down the dimly lit cement stairs that led to a cement hallway. It was dark with only the cloudy day to light it up.

“I won’t go,” Francois said.

"What is down there?" I asked.

"I don't like it down there," Charles said.

Now, I refused to go because if two survivors couldn't handle it, how could I?

In an instant, Charles grabbed my hand and latched on tightly. We walked down the stairs, hands clenched together.

It was a very narrow walkway. On both sides were wooden shelves stacked from the floor to the ceiling. On each shelf were neatly organized human skulls, machetes, and clothes from those who were murdered. The air was stale, and I immediately felt claustrophobic and sick to my stomach. What I saw took my breath away.

It's important to mention the unimaginable level of forgiveness that happens every day in Rwanda. Jadot became my greatest teacher of Rwanda's history.

"Because tens of thousands of killers were still alive, it was too many cases for our formal justice system to handle," he patiently explained to me. "As a replacement to formal trials, the communities held unification meetings called "gacacas," where the killers faced their victim's families. After begging for forgiveness, the killers were set free and lived as neighbors among the people whose family they had killed."

What he shared next was incredible.

"My dad was called to the gacaca of my older brother's killer. He was supposed to go through the motions and listen to the killer beg for forgiveness, then grant the forgiveness," Jadot shared.

What he said next made my jaw drop.

"The whole village was waiting for my dad's forgiveness. Instead, my dad looked at my brother's killer and said, 'Fuck you,' and walked away."

Before my time in Rwanda, a constant storm of combined sadness and anger from my mother's suicide raged within me. I felt like I battled it all of the time. I was mad at the mental illness that plagued my mom for most of my life. Angry that instead of bringing our family closer, we instead allowed it to divide us. Angry that the years my mom battled her depression, I grew up wondering if I would ever find her lifeless body after school. There were many times she was absent, like my high school soccer games; it was like she was a ghost in my childhood. All these repressed feelings started to rise just beneath the surface like the rumbling of hot lava just before a volcanic eruption.

In Rwanda, I mainly listened to stories. It was a consequence of not knowing the language. On some level, I knew the stories from these resilient and strong women taught me to let go of everything that was holding me back. For years, I built an emotional fortress around me, laughingly convincing myself that I'd never again feel the pain of losing someone important to me. I didn't know how to grieve, so I co-existed with that grief until it fully unraveled one afternoon in beautiful Rwanda.

It was my last day in Rwanda before returning home. I had the privilege of being invited to a meeting between artisans who had just created a new cooperative. They didn't all know each other, so they wanted to share their stories as a way of introducing themselves. I was the only "mzungu" present, and Jadot quietly translated every word as I silently sat in the back.

This was the most intense, emotional, and unbelievable afternoon I had ever experienced. The stories of survival, human indignity, and humanity's evil side led me to a deeper understanding of human pain.

"I wanted to become a nun," one woman shared. "Instead, I was impregnated by the killers. I'm HIV positive. My son is now 16, and I still can't tell him the truth about who his dad is despite his questions about his identity." She was crying now.

"I want to meet God and ask him, 'Why?!'"

Another woman said, "I tried to end my life by throwing myself down a latrine when I heard them coming. I stayed hidden for over seven days while people urinated and defecated on me. Soon I was captured."

She had seven kids by her captor, but five survived.

Another woman was only twelve when she was taken. She was so young that she didn't know what was happening to her body when she became pregnant. "I thought I had been poisoned," she said,

Women were in uncontrollable tears that wracked their bodies, moans of grief filled the room, and the sadness was suffocating. At the end of this incredible session of confessions, I broke down. I was shaking. Even though it is impossible, I felt like I could feel their pain. I wanted to squeeze the sadness and hurt out of them. I wanted to absorb it from them.

But that afternoon taught me something that changed something deep within. It changed the way I handled my own pain of not knowing how to process my chaotic feelings after the unexpected death of my mom. I learned the best thing to do is to sit with my pain. Let it run through my veins and wash over my body and soul. Let it hurt me and let it make me feel uncomfortable. Let every fiber in my body absorb it. And I realized that once I sat with the pain and let it run its course through me, that eventually, it would lessen, and there was little chance that it could return to hurt me so deeply again. This process can take days or months, or years. The timing doesn't matter—it's the way I handled it that made the difference.

"Rwanda Nziza" is a local saying meaning "Beautiful Rwanda." The popular phrase grew to have a much deeper meaning for me. The beautiful mamas of Rwanda unknowingly created a relationship where I felt safe enough to remove the high emotional barriers that I erected long ago. Barriers that gave me the false sense that I could protect myself from the tidal wave of my own pain. The problem was, the pain wasn't coming from outside of me. The devastation was felt very deep within me. I'd effectively imprisoned myself, and the strong Rwandan mamas liberated me. I finally acknowledged the lasting emotional trauma from my mom's suicide.

These loving women opened their hearts to me, and slowly, my heart opened back up, first to them, then to myself and others. I didn't know how to express emotions around the death of my mom, but I eventually learned that holding them in was keeping me in an unfulfilling life. My healing journey started with radical self-acceptance and self-love.

All the mamas helped me recapture the beauty in myself. I lost one mama but I gained 150 new mamas. I would have never found myself in Africa without my mom's passing. This powerful period in my life showed me I was living in mediocrity. Tragedy changed my life's trajectory from breaking free of the mold of a traditional life, to leading me to a place of joy, abundance, and profound meaning.

Now I am true to myself and live a liberated life—one where I love the happiness right in front of me more than the struggles way behind me.

PART 4

TAKING BACK CONTROL

JENN LAFORET

Jenn Laforet is a writer, author and founder of Write Current. With words that matter, Jenn helps women reclaim their voice.

She writes stories, guided journals and creates notebooks that connect with love and compassion—interested in deepening your connection and practice? Jenn leads her What's Blooming for You? and Journal to Reconnect programs several times per year. Each one is an invitation to reconnect and nourish your emotional body. Strengthening the opportunity for positive change for readers and journalers worldwide.

Jenn lives in Oshawa, Ontario, with her rescue dog and two children.

Fueled by coffee, laughter and enthusiasm. When Jenn's not writing in her notebooks or creating on her tablet, you can find her checking out local flower markets.

Visit Jenn online to reconnect with your powerful,
tenacious, free and playful spirit, one word at a time.

writecurrent.com

LIVING A FULLY EXPRESSED LIFE

BY: JENN LAFORET

I haven't been nice since 2016. I spent my 20s feeling like a doormat. Doing everything I was "supposed" to do—university, marriage, kids, dog, car, house, and full-time teaching job. I was on a self-imposed hamster wheel, and I was miserable. I was showing up in my life as nice instead of kind. Maybe you can relate?

When you're nice, you slip into people-pleasing, overcommitting, overscheduling. You say yes to everyone while saying no to yourself. You can't have difficult conversations with people. You'd rather hurt your own feelings than theirs. You say yes to invitations, conversations and work that doesn't light you up and end up hating it. You spend most of your time in your head, editing yourself and wondering what the perfect response is.

What do they really want to hear?

Happy? Sad? Who knows, you put a smile on your face and continue.

That was my life up until early 2015. When hearing the news of a former coworker's death made me reconsider the trajectory I was on.

I remember coming home from school that fateful day, sitting down and bawling my eyes out. Earlier that day, I found out that a woman I worked with briefly in 2012 had died of liver cancer. She was only 33. It seemed impossible that such a happy and kind person could be gone. It had never occurred to me that one day there would be no more chances.

I cried at that table because I knew if that were me, I would have major regrets. Chances not taken, dreams unfulfilled.

It took me another year to work up the courage to light a match to the life I'd so perfectly curated. I walked away from an almost decade-long teaching career and long-failing nine-year marriage in the span of 11 months.

My voice shook, and tears streamed down my face as I told Mike, "I still want to be Jillian and Christopher's mom, but I don't want to be your wife anymore."

I'd thought about getting divorced four times throughout our nine-year marriage, but I could never bring myself to say it out loud. I didn't want to see my kids less, so each time, I shook it off. "Surely, this has to get better. One day we'll be enough for each other." was on repeat in my mind. But we never were.

So on August 25, 2016, we decided to separate. This was a separation we told no one about—not even our children. We then proceeded to spend the next eleven months living separately and apart under the same roof. We never learned how to be partners; we weren't best friends or confidantes. Like two ships sailing in the night, our lives were very separate, and no one, not even our children, was the wiser.

During month six, I felt like I was drowning underwater. My best friend was travelling to Brazil and choking back tears, I asked him to please make a wish for me and toss a coin into a fountain while he was there. "I just want everything to be okay." I felt like if there was ever a place for a wish to come true, it had to be there. He obliged.

In the meantime, I set my intention that everything would be fine, even if it didn't feel like it was right now. Even when I felt like I had nowhere to turn, I kept on. As roadblocks piled up, I continued. Unwavering.

As our separation unfolded before me, years of pent-up anger, frustration and resentment that had been bubbling up beneath the surface spilled over. Once described by my ex-husband as "the nicest person he'd ever met," I felt like a stranger had invaded my body. Who was this woman?

You see, the thing about divorce is, it reveals your shadow side. The darkness that's hidden from everyone suddenly becomes something you're forced to sit with and bear witness to. To feel, and rage and cry until you are empty.

It was the first time in my life I had allowed myself to feel the full range of my anger, shame and fear. It was unfamiliar territory. This was the beginning of my conscious transformation—one in which I no longer edit my life, thoughts, or feelings.

In our marriage, Mike and I didn't see eye to eye on many things; in truth, our personalities couldn't be more opposite. We didn't have a vision for our marriage, but we chose to create one for our divorce.

After all, you don't get what you hope for. You get what you choose to consciously co-create. In the divorce, we decided to work from our vision that this experience did not have to define our children or us. Divorce did not mean failure, even if it felt like that at the time. And we didn't have to see how everything would fall into place, just trust and surrender.

To co-parent effectively, we both had to do our own inner work separately. For me, the first step when I moved out in July 2017 was redefining relationships—learning to trust myself. To set and hold boundaries because boundaries are kind, and I was done being nice.

That first year of co-parenting consisted of all drop-offs and pickups done at school. I remember telling Mike that "I wasn't ready to be his friend." I couldn't just dial everything back to 2002 when that's all we were. "We are in the business of raising children together now, Mike." That boundary pattern interrupted our relationship. It created space for a new, functional co-parenting one to unfold.

Life got better when I stopped being nice and chose to be kind. When I am kind, I set boundaries in all areas of my life. Those boundaries led to thriving relationships, friendships and work as a writer and author. Based on a foundation of mutual trust, integrity and respect. I protect my *yes* and say *no* with ease. I let people know what I am and am not available for in my life and business. Without explanation, because I do not owe anyone an apology for showing up in my own life as my authentic self.

Neither do you.

Choosing to operate from a place of trust, integrity and respect. Setting and holding boundaries—these were the first steps in consciously transforming my life.

Rippling over into my ability to co-parent with Mike. When I released the idea of what family "should" look like, we redefined our relationship from husband and wife to co-parents, and the grief subsided and healing began.

But as I would soon learn to begin to truly heal, I'd first need to receive one of the biggest lessons in divorce: to release attachment.

To get there, I had to redefine motherhood.

In my mind, at that time, I thought of a mother as someone who sees her children every day, and I don't anymore. That devastated me. A tough mindset shift to make, but I've redefined it. I'm really glad I had people in my life who held space for me during that time. Because holy hell did I need a lighthouse to see through that fog. Lighthouse friends are the best kind.

Have I accepted it?

Most days. I'd be lying, though, if I didn't marvel each time I picked them up from school on transition day, at how much taller they've grown in the five days since I last saw them.

I know its quality over quantity, but as the waves of the ocean, sometimes it takes me under.

One thing I've come to know over the past five years is that it is possible to love, cherish and celebrate your children's big moments without wrapping it in the emotion of not being there to witness it.

Like when our son Christopher achieved two big milestones at his dad's house this past spring. I got a video of him riding his bike for the first time ever with no training wheels! And his front tooth finally fell out after weeks of waiting. I face-timed him to celebrate.

Three years ago, those texts would have devastated me. I would have wrapped it in the judgement of "I wasn't there." I'm glad that I chose to reframe motherhood and family. I can now celebrate these moments with peace, love and joy.

We are all energetically connected. Our children are learning that physical presence does not equal love. Many families are physically present daily, and love is absent. Perhaps when they're older, because they know what it is to feel abundant with love, they will be able to more accurately identify its absence in their adult relationships simply because their barometer of love is not a physical presence.

You are the only person who gets to decide what you're missing out on.

Navigating major holiday celebrations for me meant releasing attachment to other people's expectations of what Christmas *should* be (can we just delete that word from our collective vocab) and focus on connection. I was finally applying the lessons my friend Karen tried to instill in me during the course of our almost seven-year friendship.

Love was her highest value. As I navigated the separation, she showed me that vulnerability was my real strength. That when I work and live from a place of love, I set and hold boundaries to guide relationships, not block them.

She never left one thing unsaid. Even if that meant telling you something you didn't want to hear, it was delivered firm with love. If she loved you, you knew it, and if she was proud of you, she'd say it every damn time. To live open-hearted and be unafraid of it was the legacy of her life.

The greatest lesson she ever taught me was to be transparent in my thoughts, words and actions. That's exactly what the next step in my healing was. I was consciously transforming my life into one that was fully expressed and unedited; the evidence was all around. I just had to look.

I was reminded of that lesson at our daughter's Christmas concert in 2019. As we waited for our daughter to take the stage, our son, who isn't in choir, sat in the audience with their dad and me. I love that even though he's six, he still wants to sit on my lap and give me tight hugs. He spent most of the concert telling me about his day. We lip-synced to Wham! *Last Christmas*, when it came on and giggled. Just like we did in the car the other day when it came on.

In the past, I would have shushed him because it's a concert. I would've felt exhausted and not been present when he was talking. "That's enough" might have crossed my lips when he went in for the 10th hug. I don't take any of that for granted anymore. I listen to the stories. Not just my kids but people I meet because we all want to be heard. I give and receive hugs better from my kids and other people too. I hug tighter and don't let go first. Most of all, I know that whether I see my kids every day or not, their eyes still light up when I walk into the room. Perhaps we love each other more deeply than we did before. More than I thought possible, and that's because I learned how to love myself.

You see, in January 2019, I made a commitment to myself that I was going to spend the year dedicated to inner work—

That I would make it the year that I truly showed up for myself.

That I could hold eye contact in the mirror and know my worth.

To love me and accept me for who I was right now.

To be grateful for my life and everything in it.

To accept where I was right now.

To be at peace with it.

Not the lip service of self-care or B.S. motivational quotes, but truly doing the work, learning how to BE.

Showing up when I didn't feel like it. When I didn't think I deserved it. When that nagging voice in my head whispered, "who do you think you are to invest in yourself?"

“To care about yourself so deeply?”

For the first time in my entire life, I made the past 12 months about me.

Do you know what happened?

Everything opened up for me.

Life isn't testing you. It's reflecting you.

You are 100% responsible for your own life.

Spending a year in Jim Fortin's transformational group coaching program was the most time I have ever invested in myself.

I'm forever grateful.

The peace, freedom and ease it brought me and the ripple effect it had in my relationships and parenting.

In 2020, four years post-separation and two years divorced, one thing is clear. We became a family. Two functional co-parents, something we never managed in our nine years of marriage.

The major lesson that blew through my late 30s was as soon as you release your illusion of control and how you think things should be is when you'll receive.

Can I tell you a secret? My version of how I thought things should be was never as great as it turned out when I let things just BE and unfold as they're meant to.

We are always growing and expanding. Relationships change, roles change, work changes, friendships change.

I'm grateful for it all.

Last year, on the evening before my 40th birthday. My ex-husband and children made me a cake, a beautiful dinner and gave me one of my favourite types of flowers.

"They didn't have Callas, Jenn, so I went with Gerberas because I know how much you love them," Mike said.

Family was the word that sprung to mind. I smiled as I blew out the candles, knowing that the wish I made when I was pregnant on my 30th birthday had come true. It all unfolded as it was meant to.

Separate and apart, we are a family.

In the divorce, I learned that I am safe to feel and express the full range of my feelings. That I will not buckle under their weight.

My relationship with Mike was a growth relationship that put me on the path of standing in my personal power and owning who I am unapologetically. An invitation to peel my mask off in divorce and own who I am and what I want to co-create in my life. It was painful but necessary.

It's important to share with people what they bring to your life. I told Mike that I love what he brings with laughter. He has always been someone who wants people to have a good time and just to keep things very surface level. I crave the depth of conversations, feelings, emotions. I want to know it all. The good, bad and ugly, I have the capacity for sharing space with them all. Most importantly, when I choose to feel them, I can move through and release them, something I wasn't willing to do for most of my life.

When I tapped into my own feelings, I realized just how powerfully I could feel other people's feelings and energy. How intuitive I am and how I had shut it down because it scared me. It is a gift that I received when I learned how to FEEL and ALLOW the dark and the light because that's where love is, in the darkest and lightest corners of ourselves.

That's part of living a fully expressed life. Not everyone has the capacity for that. He has the capacity to hold the good and always lets the good times roll. He loves his friends. Now that I'm one of them (friendship in our divorce was a gift that came with time, space and healing), he can relate to me in a more positive way.

These days, my friendships and relationships are fueled by different things—love, respect, trust, passion, purpose, impact, and laughter.

But I do have reverence and appreciation for people who show up and love me in the way that they best know-how while also respecting the boundaries that have been set and held. For him, that has always been "let me make light of something".

When I don't wrap that in judgement, I can appreciate it and him better. I am fully seeing him and accepting him as he is.

Oprah says true forgiveness is when you can look at someone and say thank you for the experience.

Thank you for the experience, Mike.

More importantly, thank you to both of us for releasing with peace and love so that we could evolve this relationship five years ago and turn into a family, separate and apart, on our own terms.

When you hold onto relationships you've outgrown that aren't aligned with your highest values or vision of your life, you block yourself from living a fully expressed life.

Glad we are both free to attract a partner to adventure through life with.

I am grateful that we still get to be special guest stars in each other's lives. That's how we show up best for each other and our children.

Release.

Don't block your flow.

When you allow yourself to release and receive, you step into living a fully expressed life, one with relationships that are co-created, rooted in trust, integrity and respect with:

Nothing left unsaid.

Nothing left unfelt.

Nothing left undone.

Allow yourself to invite and receive these new people, opportunities and experiences into your life with gratitude and joy. The universe always knows what you need and makes sure it unfolds when you have the awareness and boundaries to receive well.

Married: Nine years and Divorced: Two years

"The world is this way or that way because I tell myself the world is this way or that way," a saying I've heard many times by one of my mentor's Jim Fortin.

On July 7, 2020, Mike and I celebrated our "Un-Anniversary" with steak, lobster and a dart game with our kids.

I got a bullseye, and I do not just *understand* that lesson that Jim shared. I *know* it.

It's not lost on me that I abandoned my sense of self when I got married on July 7, 2007.

The universe knew it and returned me to me, signed, sealed and delivered 11 years later.

Same exact date.

A universal energy reset for both of us to return to ourselves, reclaim our personal power and step into our true selves.

Separate and apart as it should be.

We each abandoned our true selves in that marriage.

What does it cost someone to be in a relationship with you?

In our marriage, the price was never being our true selves and dimming our respective lights. Playing small in life and love in hopes we could force it to work.

We didn't believe we deserved better back then when we were in the thick of it.

Surely this must get better was the mantra I shared earlier and it never did until we released with peace and love and evolved the relationship in divorce. That price was steep, and I have pictures of myself with vacant eyes for many years because of it.

We each created a wasteland of self-abandonment with so much of our true selves scattered to the wind and given up as we tried to fit a square peg in a round hole.

An example of the universe, allowing us to exercise free will by entering that marriage together but ultimately knowing better and resetting it because the universe has the final say.

I am grateful.

The universe keeps perfect records and that was the catalyst of my self-love journey.

It is a lifelong commitment to myself to show up for myself first with love, trust, integrity and respect.

I am peace.

I am calm.

I am love.

So are you.

Healing doesn't just happen overnight. It takes time and is an ongoing process. It's not like one day you wake up, and you're like, "yes! I'm healed." But day by day, sometimes moment to moment, it's happening.

The best way I can describe it is like the waves of the ocean. Sometimes you're playing and jumping over them with ease. Other times, you lose your footing, and they knock you down. You stand up breathless, with a tear-stained face, but that wave didn't get you. And so you get back to jumping over and playing in them. Sometimes with a helping hand from the people who love you and share space with you as you heal.

When you work from circumstance, your options are limited. When you work from possibility - thc world is at your feet.

Change seems impossible. Transforming a relationship can be scary, but you owe it to yourself to live a fully expressed life.

I hope you choose to see possibility over circumstance - I'll be here cheering you on.

LIZ JAKOI

Liz believes life is meant to be lived to the fullest, liberated from limitations. She teaches you to become the self-leader of your mind, body and soul.

We tend to see things from a limited perspective, especially during times of stress, anxiety and depression. Liz helps you to unpack the thinking that is holding you back so you can see more possibilities.

Are you ready to see beyond where you are today?

Liz graduated from University in Toronto with a degree in Psychology and with a minor in Philosophy. She worked in the corporate world in Human Resources, Training and Development, and as a Job Coach/Counsellor. After conducting 100s of workshops and counselling 100s of people on how to design a new life after a major life event, Liz decided in 2017, that she could really serve people best by starting her own business.

In February 2014, at the of age 56, Liz had her third breakdown. Her first one was in her 20s after losing her father to cancer and then leaving her first marriage. Her second one was in her 30s when she was getting remarried and her job was declared redundant.

For most of her life, living was painful. She wanted to die. She was either stressed, anxious and depressed, or calm in the chaos. When she fought the battle the first 2 times, everything returned to normal. She lived to fight another day – another battle. She spent most of her time assuring everyone that she was fine and stronger than before only to be overwhelmed by both her past and her future. This time, she decided to fight to *become Liz*; to live a life outside of being a mother, daughter, employee, wife and friend.

After spending decades of living in a constant state of stress, anxiety and depression, Liz is now grounded, calm, and strong. As a Holistic Transformational Coach and Facilitator, Liz draws out the strategies you are using that keep you stuck, and helps you develop new strategies so that you can shine your light brightly.

Through her coaching sessions, you get comfortable with being uncomfortable about making changes to your life strategies that no longer serve you.

Liz Jakoi helps businesswomen who feel overloaded by the stress of juggling work, family life and aging parents to reconnect with their inner warrior in order to take control of their lives by getting clarity, confidence and elevate their personal and professional experiences.

lizjakoi@gmail.com

www.lizjakoi.com

https://www.linkedin.com/in/lizjakoi

TAKE CHARGE OF YOUR LIFE

BY: LIZ JAKOI

Emotional fitness is just as important as physical fitness. Today, I am a transformed woman, mind, body, and soul. I am a speaker, author and transformation facilitator helping women reconnect to their inner warrior to live a meaningful and fulfilling life. Why do I do this? Ever since I was a little girl growing up in Toronto, I was always curious about the inner workings of the human mind and felt compelled to be a teacher. When I started my education at the University of Toronto with a major in Psychology and a minor in Philosophy, I was really looking at getting a better understanding of my own mind and what makes human beings behave the way they do. I was divorced from my first husband in 1991 and I was engaged to be married again in 1994. My journey to conscious transformation started in 1993 when my Human Resources Advisor position at the Liquor Control Board of Ontario was declared redundant. I was crushed, deflated, and took it personally. I began to study meditation, devouring dozens of personal development books that helped me crawl out of the hole I was in. Then family duties and responsibilities put things on hold until 2010, when I began to study the law of attraction. Over the last few years, I've been studying neuroscience to understand how the brain works and spirituality, which has really transformed my life. My company began in 2017, initially focusing on physical health and nutrition. I decided to expand my business in 2018 to coach private clients on mindset and teach them what I had learned. As a transformational warrior, the tools I use have helped me create exceptional results for myself and have had a meaningful impact on my life. I see us as warriors, battling the limiting mental, emotional, physical, and thinking patterns by using laser-sharp coaching, combining neuroscience, the law of attraction and psychology to make shifts in living our true potential.

THINK IT

So let me take you back a few years to when my conscious transformation started. It was 2014; I was 56 years of age and had my third breakdown. I had my first in my 20's, then my 30's and now, the walls came crumbling down. For most of my life, I have been battling stress, anxiety, overwhelm and depression. Ever since I was a teenager, I learned that it was best to keep it hidden from my friends and even my family. I kept it hidden because it wasn't safe to talk about feelings, especially when I was "down." It could also be the way I was raised. My mom would gently tell me not to cry; everything was going to be okay. Deep down inside my heart, I knew my mom meant well. She did not want me to be in pain. It was her way to help me feel better. "You just have to keep going, sweetie; everything is going to be okay," she would say to me.

That is pretty much how I lived my life. On the outside, I was a high-functioning person who appeared to have it all together. I participated in sports, had boyfriends throughout high school, had fun when I went out with friends, went to school, got a degree, started a career, got married, got divorced, dated, got married again, had two kids—everything was fine. Just keep going.

Driving home from work on a cold, snowy evening, I thought this is not how I envisioned my life. I'm not as far along as I should be. I'm not fulfilling my destiny or dreams. I couldn't take it anymore. I was in so much emotional pain. Nothing I tried seemed to help. The counsellors, therapists, self-help books, law of attraction, nothing!

Up ahead, in the bend of the road, I saw this huge willow tree and thought to myself, what would happen if I just put the pedal to the metal and wrapped my car around the tree. Instantaneously, I thought about my teenage kids. I did not want to leave them with *him*. Even though they were 14 and 17, they still needed me. He was disengaged and was not the father or husband I thought he would be when we were dating. We talked about shared parenting, household chores, and our dreams of retiring and growing old together. How did these things change so quickly after my firstborn?

Later that evening, I was lying in bed, and I began to think to myself. How did I get here? What led up to this? Why does this keep happening to me? Why do I feel good for a while, and then *bam*, something happens, and I feel like I'm in quicksand?

This wasn't the first time I contemplated suicide. When I was 18, I called the suicide hotline. I wanted to die. All I knew was that I was in a lot of pain. I couldn't understand what or why I was thinking and feeling like I wanted to end my life. For years I had been anxious and depressed, kept it all inside, and it was becoming unbearable. I was scared because my feelings and thinking were out of control. I didn't know how to stop. I wanted to fight, run away, and then I felt paralyzed. I had no idea how to deal with these emotions and thoughts. Somehow, deep down inside, I knew that wanting to end my life was not rational. Part of me knew that I still had my whole life ahead of me. It didn't feel safe to talk to my friends and family about it or get support from anyone. I heard my friends and family talk about people who had anxiety or depression. They were very dismissive, apathetic, and judged people without showing understanding or compassion. They would say things like, "They should just snap out of it", "It could be worse" or "They think they have it bad, well just the other day…." and "They are selfish.". Being selfish stood out in my mind the most.

I stayed silent, buried my emotions, and just lived to get through the day. It's taken me decades to realize that I am a high-functioning depressed person. More recently, the characteristics I have lived all my life fall under Persistent Depressive Disorder. On the outside, I was powering through and appeared to be handling life's curveballs. For me, life was like being sucked into this quicksand and the more I struggled to find ways to ease the pain of not being good enough, the deeper into the quicksand I felt I sank. I appeared to be fine, but inside, I was dying.

In the winter of 2014, my life was a mess. I was working full-time as an Employment Facilitator and Counsellor, my marriage of 24 years was loveless, my mom was diagnosed with Alzheimer's, and my kids were constantly sick. I was juggling doctor's appointments, work, home, activities and looking after ageing parents on both sides. That morning of the near-fatal night, my boss called me into his office. He told me that I was overloaded and taking way too much time away to attend doctor's appointments, which was not sustainable; not only because of the disruption it caused in the workplace, but also for me personally. If I continued down this path, I could end up six feet under. What would happen to my kids then? I broke down sobbing in his office because I knew he was right. Things had to change. I had to change.

When my kids were 8 and 5 years old, I remember driving around looking at townhouses and imagining what life would be like if I left with the kids. We could have our own little townhouse, which would give them room to play in the backyard. I felt so free, so alive, so happy thinking about leaving my husband. Then the reality of not having money and not knowing what to do hit home. I had no "paying" job because I was a stay-at-home Mom. I had no idea how to leave. But, as usual, the voices from the past emerged. Marriage is work. Nobody is perfect. You must work at it. So, I returned home and decided to keep working at it. I tried everything to get my husband to engage with our kids—therapists, counsellors, self-help books, googling information on the web. I shared the info I found with him. We coordinated weekends where he would have alone time with one child, and I would have alone time with the other child. Then we would switch. This only lasted a couple of months because I decided that I would wait and see if he took the initiative to ask what the plans were for the weekend. I was accused of "making decisions," so I asked him to choose. Nothing happened.

We tried about five different therapists and counsellors. He always found something he did not like about the therapist, and all I heard during therapy was all the things I do that are wrong.

When our firstborn was six months old, I asked if there was one day on the weekend that I could have to sleep in—one day on the weekend where he could wake up and look after the baby so that I could sleep in. His response was, "I need my sleep." I was hurt and felt like a dagger was plunged into my heart. I sat there stunned but did not show it. I knew I could not say anything in response because that would make things worse. He would get angry and say something even more hurtful, so I stayed silent.

I was accused of being dismissive, not listening, making decisions, using metaphors, getting emotional and defensive whenever he tried to "talk" to me about how he felt. I got emotional and defensive because I always felt it was my fault. When I tried to bring up situations and things that bothered me, he would say that every time we talk, everything turned out to be about me. I looked at it as an opportunity to air my differences, things that bothered me as well, but I was just supposed to sit there, listen to him and change my approach because he was hurting. I kept thinking to myself, what about me? What about how I feel? What about all the pain, hurt, and anger I was feeling? I was growing resentful, assuming I had to bury it deep down inside, again.

Over the years, I stayed because I felt trapped. When I complained to my mom or friends, they would tell me that he was such a nice guy. He provides for the family. Try to make him feel happy; he is the man of the house. But I knew that I couldn't make him feel satisfied. All I could do was not rock the boat, so he didn't get angry, sulk or disengage further. I ended up walking on eggshells. I tried to look at all the good qualities and focus on them. But when it came time to ask him for assistance, he would get angry and respond that I did not ask nicely or that I was dictating or commanding. Deep down inside, I knew that I had tried my best to be polite, phrase my words and use a friendly tone. Requests for help came from a scared place which he may have picked up on. Nothing seemed to work.

I thought if we went away on family vacations to Jamaica, Disney World, Universal, and the Dominican Republic, that it would provide us with the opportunity to reconnect as a family. While on holidays, it was so much work to always make sure not only the kids were happy but that he was happy too. Maki ng sure that everyone was heard in terms of what they wanted to do and where to eat. Nothing seemed to make him happy.

Driving home that near-fatal night made me realize that I had to do something. I could no longer pretend that everything was okay.

Every morning, I would wake up hoping to just get through the day. I was in survival mode. The list of things that needed to get done kept me going. Responsibility to family gave me a routine and focus on serving others kept me from sinking deeper. Or so I thought. Little did I realize that this "keep going" mentality was incredibly taxing and exhausting. I would start an exercise regime that made me feel good, and then I stopped. Read personal development books and began to feel better. Most of the things that we try are outside ourselves. Focus on the outcomes, what you want to have. Do what you need to do, and then you will be successful, happy, and content. That is a broken system, yet that is what we are taught when it comes to our businesses, life, career, personal growth, and education.

My brain was in such a fog, and I knew I was barely surviving. It felt like my brain, and my body were shutting down. I was lucky if I got 3-4 hours of sleep a night. My Irritable Bowel Syndrome was a constant battle as well, which I ignored. It didn't help that I would turn to a glass of wine or two and finish the bottle. This helped numb the racing mind and dull the pain.

Moving forward to March 2014. I sat the family down and told them what my boss had told me just a few days before. Things needed to change, and I needed to change. I told them that there were a couple of scenarios my boss thought might help me to continue working and look after the family. My kids right away said, "Quit Mom and take care of you." I said that I would have to discuss it with their father. Later that evening, we sat down, and I told him what the options were. I told him that I was drowning, barely surviving to the point where I couldn't even think. I was beyond burning out. He sat there, in silence. The silence was unnerving. I felt frustrated and overwhelmed because he was not communicating or even having a conversation about what was going on or what to do next.

We slept on it and I asked him again the next day, what his thoughts were. Silence. No response. I mentioned that the only option for now was for me to quit my job so that I could look after my Mom, his parents, the family and myself. Once everyone settles, then I could return to work. I asked him for his input. No response.

I quit my job and began my journey to transform my life and connect to who I am. My marriage was broken beyond repair. I was broken but not beyond repair.

The first year I spent resting, meditating, looking after my mom and arranging to have her put on a list for a long-term care facility. I took the time to be truly present with my kids and my mom.

I started to be aware of my thoughts and feelings and how I was in this victim consciousness for decades. I blamed the cookies in the cupboard for my weight gain. Diets don't work. It's his fault for not working on the marriage. My kids make me angry.

I realized that this was no longer working for me and that I had to make changes from the inside out.

January of 2016, I was sitting in a comfy chair, gazing out the window into the backyard. The snowflakes were huge and gently falling. I began to dream. I dreamed about travelling to Europe. How wonderful it would be to walk the cobblestone streets of Italy and visit my cousins in Budapest, Hungary. I realized that I was 80 pounds overweight, prediabetic, facing coronary disease, could barely walk without pain in my left knee because of a torn ligament, and I had no money. I thought I was too old to lose weight now and that my metabolism was shot. How many times have I tried to lose weight? I had been on a roller coaster of losing weight and gaining more weight back.

I decided that no matter what, I was going to try one more time. This time I was going to focus on getting fit. I remembered that all the other times when I worked out or played tennis, I not only felt energized physically, but it helped me emotionally as well. I joined a gym and hired a personal trainer. I started visualizing and meditating every day how I wanted to be.

By July of 2016, I lost 80 pounds and was in the best shape of my life. Not only was I feeling better physically, but my prediabetic indicators were also dissolved, I no longer felt like I was facing coronary disease and the torn meniscus slowly healed. I felt like I was in better shape than in my 20's.

In 2017, a friend approached me to join me in her fitness and nutrition business. As I started to gain momentum in the business, I became stressed and overwhelmed. Other emotional and limiting beliefs started surfacing. I had new demons to battle. I couldn't understand what was happening. I felt great the past year with conquering my physical health and was feeling so much better mentally.

On April 1, 2017, my husband approached me and said he wanted a separation. I agreed. I remember the look of shock on his face. Secretly, I thought about ending the marriage. I did not include him in any of my dreams or visions.

The next few months, we spent visiting lawyers and working through the financial process. I remember how overwhelming and difficult it was to complete paperwork and attend the meetings. I started to see that selling the matrimonial home would give me the money to buy the townhouse for me and the kids I had been dreaming about for over ten years. The universe responds when the time is right.

CHANGE IT

So how did I climb out of this quicksand?

First, Decide. Decide on what you want. The next step is focusing on who we want to be. Next, think about what that means for you and how you are going to feel.

When I was 14, I was diagnosed with degenerative disc disease and arthritis. I was told to stop playing sports because I could sustain injury to my spinal cord and be paralyzed. I decided that I was going to continue playing sports. It made me happy and feel confident. Sports was my lifeline. Because of that decision, I am active and have 2 kids even though I have advanced degenerative discs and chronic arthritis.

What this taught me was that, once you decide that you are not going to allow your condition or circumstances to dictate how your life is going to play out, you can do and achieve anything you want in life.

Next, I started to think about my thinking. Paying attention to my thoughts. What am I thinking? What I am thinking when I am walking up the stairs, when I am in the grocery lineup, when I am in the shower and most importantly when I am driving the car. I became aware of how horribly I spoke about myself. The negative self-talk was on this loop, repeating itself over and over. The thoughts that I would have about people, how they wronged me, how horrible they were. Negative thoughts about my husband, my kids not listening and not doing chores.

After becoming aware of my thoughts, I started to pay attention to how I was feeling.

For decades, I ignored my feelings, bottled them up and just kept ploughing through. I had this pit in my stomach, felt nauseous, like I was going to vomit. Instead of cancelling social activities now, I acknowledge the feeling and journal my thinking.

When I got really stressed, I would feel this tightness in my chest and my breathing would be quick. Sometimes I could feel my heart beating faster. I paid attention to my wanting to fight or flee, to when I would freeze or become paralyzed and unable to move. I now breathe and investigate my thinking.

When I felt this tight band around my head, I acknowledged that I was in a deep state of overwhelm. I began to pay attention to what I was feeling and linking it to my thinking.

I remember when I was in the lawyer's office beginning the initial stages of my separation and my throat felt tight and sore. My eyes were welling up with tears as I was fighting back the urge to cry. My lawyer asked if I was okay and if I wanted to stop. I said, "No, let's keep going. I need to keep going." I remember paying attention to the voices in my head telling me, "You're a sissy," "You're just being manipulative," "Those are just crocodile tears." These are things that I heard from my past, my ex-husband, my parents, and I knew I had to somehow wipe them out of my mind.

I started turning things around by telling myself I had a right to cry because I was afraid of what was going to happen next. I had no job, no income, and no money. What was I going to do about my kids? I had to take them with me. I had no idea what I was going to do next. I decided that leaving this loveless, emotionally abusive marriage was the first step. I needed to get clear on what I was going to do. What was the next step? What action could I take to make this happen?

I started to think about what I wanted this next chapter to look like, this next half or stage of my life.

I decided that I wanted to climb out of the quicksand once and forever. I did some research on what to do if you were actually in quicksand and followed a similar method.

1. They say to lighten your load when in quicksand. Get rid of a backpack and find ways to get lighter. I started to lighten the heaviness of this stress, anxiety, overwhelm and depression by asking myself empowering questions. Questions that made me feel good, confident, and secure, and helped me gain momentum.
2. Just like quicksand, they suggest taking small steps backward. I decided that taking a few steps backward would get me on solid ground by seeing where I came from. This would help me become optimistic about the progress I've made in other areas of my life, by looking

at how far I have come instead of only looking at the negative. This helped me focus on the future.

3. When in quicksand, they tell you to keep your arms and head up above the surface. I began yoga, which gave me fluidity of movements and also helped me to stay in the moment.
4. Find resources to help you and pull you out. I hired personal trainers for my mind and body. They helped me assess my situation and would be there to grab hold of me whenever I felt I was sinking again and to pull me out as necessary. I hired business and mindset coaches and received certifications.
5. I learned the power of breathing and meditation to keep me in a state of calm. Just like in quicksand, this helps you stay buoyant.
6. While you are working on freeing your legs in quicksand, with every inch you move upward toward the surface, you allow for a moment for the quicksand to fill the space it once occupied. When freeing yourself from negative thinking and the bad feelings associated with it, allow positive thinking and positive feelings to fill the space where the negative feelings were. Depending on how deep you have sunk, this process could take days, weeks, months. Patience is the key and taking quick giant steps can reverse your progress.

The biggest thing I learned was harnessing the power of slowing down and taking my time. Moving slowly and deliberately enabled me to have clarity and focus.

Once I set my intention and decided on what I wanted to do, things started to fall into place.

LIVE IT

By August of 2017, I suggested to my ex that we needed to sit down and tell the kids. He just stared at me. I said "We need to do this soon and together. If we don't do it by August 15, I will do it myself." On August 16, 2017, I first told my son that Dad and I were separating. My son responded by saying, "It's about time." I was stunned. I asked him what he meant by that. He said, "Mom, you have not been happy for years." I told him I tried to hide my pain about my marriage and just focus on him and his sister. He said that I didn't do a very good job. I laughed, thinking that we try to hide what is ailing us and sometimes we wear our heart on our sleeves. Later that day, I told my daughter, and she said, "Good." She said we could Snapchat each other when on dates.

The separation was progressing at a snail's pace. He was still living in the matrimonial home on the advice of his lawyer. In February of 2018, I had my gallbladder removed and my daughter had a funny mole removed from her toe. Although I had bought groceries before my procedure, we were running out of some things. I made a list of groceries. I explained that I couldn't drive for five days and wondered if he could pick up some groceries for us. He responded by saying that he didn't feel like it because I commanded it and didn't ask nicely. When I responded by saying that I thought I did ask nicely, he told me that I was dismissing him and his feelings. It was a no-win situation. This was how he responded throughout the 24 years. I decided early on that I had to do everything myself. It wasn't much longer now.

In March 2018, his Mom fell and ended up in the hospital. He decided to move out and move into her home so that he could look after her when she came out of thc hospital. Hc didn't even tell the kids he was moving out. He just left. She passed away in July. I felt like I had lost my mom because I looked after her. I took her grocery shopping every week and made sure one of her sons took her to doctor's appointments. When the obituary came out, we noticed there was no mention of me. But I learned that being free from him was all that mattered.

After I healed from the gallbladder removal, I decided to enter a fitness competition. The competition was held during a summit in Indianapolis. I knew that would help me stay positive and focused on what I needed to do.

The kids and I moved into our new townhome, and in August 2018, we went to Budapest, Hungary to visit my cousins and celebrate milestones. I had turned 60 in May, my daughter was 21 in May, and my son was 18 in July. That comfy couch moment 2 years ago was manifesting, and I was beginning to feel like my life was fulfilling.

The process of conscious transformation is a continuous process. It is a lifestyle, a lifelong pursuit. Much like going to the gym to build our muscles. We don't just go for a few months and stop. Continuous movement of some kind is critical for our muscles or we lose strength, endurance, as well as bone density, and metabolism.

Our brain is very similar. We have this amazing muscle between our ears that houses the technology of our being. Pills and devices cannot make changes to the neuro networks that maintain mental and emotional fitness. Only you or I can guide and direct changes to our brain through upgrading the software on a continuous basis. I believe we learn from womb to tomb.

'Living it' means having a daily ritual to start your day and taking charge when you notice you are in a negative state mentally and emotionally.

My daily ritual includes gratitude, meditation, visualization, exercise and personal development.

Whenever I get anxious or overwhelmed, I begin to breath and picture my life as I want it to be. This gives me clarity, focus and calm confidence to keep moving forward.

There was a time where I wanted to die, I contemplated suicide. Now I realize, that was the beginning of my transformation.

I still see that willow tree in the bend of the road, now and again. But now when I see that tree, I don't want to hurt myself or the tree. I see that tree as a symbol. That tree is a pillar of strength. For decades, it has withstood Mother Nature's battles, and the sun still shines on that tree. I began to look at how much life is like that. Battling inner demons and outside demons, yet the sun still shines on us. Sometimes I can't see the forest for the trees but I do see that willow tree.

I am who I am today because of all the battles that I have fought. Changing my life from the inside out saved me and helped me to take charge of my life.

FRAN STEYN

Born & raised in Johannesburg, South Africa, Fran moved to Canada in 2002 and began her business first known as Frantastic Treats over 12 years ago, baking holiday sugar cookies with her gifted stand mixer in her North York apartment. Today this Social Entrepreneur, and award-winning Boss Lady owns a multi-location foodie business located in Oshawa, Ontario, with her newest location in the Oshawa Centre.

Fran and her husband Jonathan chose Whitby as their families' home in 2011 just before their second son was born. With the goal of working, living, and playing close to home – Whitby as a home and business community has become her absolute dream come true.

Fran and her dedicated and talented team at Frantastic have been proudly serving Durham Region community with their wide variety of savoury, unique, gourmet treats and meals; including Keto/Gluten Free/Low Carb & Naturally Sweetened meals; soups; bakery items and desserts. They also offer online cooking and baking classes and parties. Their innovative food creations have positioned their business as a sought-after caterer and food destination in Durham Region.

Daily, you can find Fran managing her foodie empire, snapping pictures and posting tons of social media, on her food truck, in the kitchen, or bouncing around to her different locations. Food has always been her passion, as is her love of the business of *business*.

IF YOU DON'T TRY, YOU WILL NEVER KNOW

BY: FRAN STEYN

"If you don't try, you will never know."

I am not sure when or where I learned this belief, but I have felt this way as far back as I can remember. It could have been one of those moments of encouragement given by my Mom – she always said just the right thing to make me feel like I could achieve anything – as a child, and still now.

Thinking back to the first part of my journey leaving South Africa, in retrospect, I have been on a journey of transformations my whole life. Anyone who has taken the leap of emigration will understand how one does, in fact, leave an entire life behind – a whole other version of self, which does not exist anymore, like a death that must be mourned.

The interesting starting point of my story is that I was raised by two entrepreneurial parents. When I was asked at school what my parents did, my response was always met with confusion by kids who had never heard the term. They had always worked for themselves (well, during my life anyway), so it was very interesting that I had chosen to study Psychology and Education. Fast-forward, a lot of history and emigrating from South Africa to Canada – where my first sales job happened (not my first job, just my first job in sales). I had always had a philosophical view on life; in my mind, objects could never hold any actual value, and therefore, I could never "sell" anything as a job or career. My experience selling an awesome brand of kitchen knives was a low-risk attempt for me. They told me I would get paid even if I didn't sell anything. And as I went through the motions, I could not believe how people actually wanted to buy this product from me. I felt as if I had won the lottery each time. I soon figured out that people believed me because I believed in the product. I REALLY believed in the product, so much so that I had the entire set for myself. That was when the absolute THRILL of sales and a love for the business of business was born for me. Within three months, I was coaching new sales reps on their selling technique, and I was offered a management position, which I turned down, knowing this was not a long-term goal for me.

Perhaps a little background information might fill in some gaps. In 2002, when I was 22 years old, I left South Africa for a fantastic work/travel opportunity. I came to Canada as an *au pair* under the Live-In Caregiver program and was able to complete my 2nd-year Psychology Honours Degree through the University of South Africa, here in Canada. Perfect opportunity for me to travel a bit, see the world, and return home. Well, needless to say, that did not happen; 2021 will be a celebration of 19 years living in Canada – almost as many years living here as I had there. I still get asked the same question – "So do you like it here"? Yes, of course, I like it here, hello…? 19 years!! And yes, I do miss where I came from and a whole life that was left behind – however Canada turned out to be a whole lot of adventure that deserves its own book!

I completed my BA degree in Psychology, Sociology, Education and Criminology in South Africa. After three years as an au pair, I worked in child care programming, retail, floral design and décor. I completed an Early Childhood Educator equivalency, qualified to teach English as a Second Language, and completed a year of Post-Secondary graduate studies in Art Therapy. (Insert deep breath here) – I know the list is exhausting, even to type – but this was my journey and how I began to develop a life for myself and build every inch of my future here in Canada.

In retrospect, I would say that I had a whole lot of interest in a whole lot of stuff. I still feel that way – there are so many fields that bring me joy – which is probably why the more that is going on in my world, the happier I am. Hence, the life of an entrepreneur.

Starting my baking business around 13 years ago, from home, was an attempt at making some extra income – without having to get another job. I was already married at that point in my life but didn't have my boys yet. We worked an insane amount of hours to build our lives. At one point, I was a Preschool Teacher, Assistant Manager at a children's clothing store; tutored English as a second language and worked for a party décor company. When I started my baking business, I had just had my first son, and instead of going back to work as a preschool teacher, I decided to try a home daycare, which was my first taste of running my own show and owning a home business. It turned out to be quite a profitable situation, and I was so grateful to be able to spend that time with my child and earn an income at the same time.

What started out as a hobby baking business for me – transformed into more as time went on, with people asking for random baked items and stores asking for a product to sell. When we moved to Whitby, and my second son was 3 months old – I decided to open Frantastic Events (yes, I said 3 months old - insert crazy person face here) – the bricks and mortar version – and begin growing my catering company. February 14th, 2021 – mid-Pandemic – I just celebrated 9 years in business!

Let me just pause here to insert – the complete creation and growth of my business from the ground up took 24-7-365 for me, blood, sweat, and so, so, so many tears - sometimes through the nights. In absolutely no way would I want to minimize this process, or make it seem like it was "Peaches & Cream," it was not; it was hard, so hard I often wondered if I was going to make it through. I cannot describe how my husband who also had a full time sales job, on the road all the time and his own version of career goals stepped up into Super Dad so that I could chase my dream. I do not know if our house would have remained standing or if the children would have been fed, or if we would have clean clothes on a daily basis, but I never had to worry. He did it all. When I could not. He did. Growing a business does NOT happen alone. You need support. Family, friends, people who will remind you just how amazing you are – when you do not see it at ALL.

At the beginning it was all me, all the time. I do not think 3500 words could begin to scratch the surface of the journey I have been through to get to this point - with two locations and a food truck, six staff members and a whole lot of business going on.

I think as time goes on, some things have changed and many things have remained the same.

The kinds of things I am passionate about start out with my love for all things food and being of service to others; definitely the business of business is at the very top of the list. The psychologist in me always thinks about and analyses consumer buyer behaviour and the effects of persuasion in the sales process. The opportunity to teach in any situation brings me so much joy, when I was approached to teach Introduction to Business at Durham College about four years ago – I jumped at the opportunity. Never having formally studied business, this was an amazing opportunity for me to gain that insight that I always wondered about and help others understand the business of business. I could only teach for three semesters, with my business on a mega growth curve, but I think I will return to that level of teaching someday.

Details like scaling, logistics, planning and execution of my catered events has become a true passion for me as time has gone on and my business has evolved. From inception to completion, mapping out the plan and getting it all done gives me ultimate joy!

One year ago, I began an incredible project—a Social Entrepreneurship charitable mission called Souptastic. Through public nomination and community support and partnerships, we give free soup and a bun to nominees. This has given me an amazing glimpse into a legacy that I can create that will exist beyond myself. Little did I know or begin to understand how valuable this would be over the last year through the Covid crisis, as I quickly used this concept to reach out to the elderly, isolated and immune-compromised individuals in our community through this soup giving program. We also provided thousands of meals to front line workers in Health Care as well as government and all levels of service providers.

I was meant to have this story published in a book a year ago, but I was not able to complete it. Two major things happened in my world, which changed the trajectory of my life forever – the first, and most obvious was the outbreak of the Covid-19 pandemic. At the point of writing this,we have been in this time warp for over a year already, and I am so grateful to have the opportunity to write this down in my story, as I feel it is a momentous time to be alive and to be able to share this story. However, the second and even more painful reason, is that in August last year, my father took his own life. Now, while I do not at all feel it is necessary to describe any of that in detail, I feel that was a point of transformation for me. My life changed forever that day, and moving forward I will never be the same.

Transformation – the ability to change, adapt "pivot" (ugh, this has become an overused term of the worldwide business pandemic terminology) – how about we just refer to it as SURVIVE, and then to THRIVE once again? This is all about flexibility. Being open to change. Being open. Using what you already have, and what you already know - to solve new problems that exist.

Yes, I have transformed; I have transformed my entire business. I transformed a primarily in-person catering service that was dedicated to in person corporate gatherings (with the volume that we may not see at all for the foreseeable future), into a meal prepping and home delivery service, with a strong online event platform offering workshops and parties. I have shut down two of four of my locations due to Covid-19 and have had to deal with the 3rd location in a mall open and close and open and close again – as the restrictions adjust based on numbers and lockdowns.

During this time, I have pushed forward to work on wholesaling my keto specialty products. My latest vision is focussing on all my personal joys and gifts in one place. Food, teaching and my ability to inspire others. I am working on a kids cooking series to help foster confidence and self esteem in children - while mastering tasks in the kitchen.

Yes, I have transformed – I have also become more of the mother I have always wanted to be. I have been given the gift of the home school environment. The past year has given me time. Time, at home, with my children. Watching them. Watching them learn, grow, think and be. They say things to me, like "I remember when it used to always be Dad around all the time, and now it's you." OR "Aren't you more of a hands-on boss? Why are you home so much?" OR "Will you be working from home today?"

My beliefs, core values and goals have transformed. Some are clearer and some still change daily. Honestly, I am still navigating through it all, but one thing is for sure, I am very grateful for all this time to grow. What a journey—pain and all.

ACKNOWLEDGMENTS

As always, this book would not have been made possible without the incredible women and man who courageously shared their stories throughout the pages of this book. I know it was not easy, and it was difficult to relive some of your painful past. I am DEEPLY grateful for the honour and privilege to share your words in Conscious Transformation.

And to our amazing book coach Danielle Scruton who always shows up fully for our authors. Guiding them and providing writing support to help them turn their stories into their chapter. For her expert editing skills to make this book ready for our wonderful readers. I am thankful to have you here on this journey.

I also want to thank our other amazing editor, Joya Williams. For her consistent support in being another set of eyes editing the book further, to help it get publish ready. I am beyond grateful for your support.

I also want to say a HUGE THANK YOU to my Business Manager Micha Magpantay, without whose help and support this project and many projects in my business would be a million times harder to execute. Thank you for your organization, detail and support in keeping this project moving forward. I am forever grateful to have you as part of my team!

As always, I am forever grateful for my family, whom whenever I take on a new project, like this book, had to share my attention and focus. Thank you for being my constant love and support. The place I call home.

To my sisters and mom, for your love and support my whole life. I am truly blessed! To my kids, I love you. I am a better woman because of you. You are my greatest teachers and the reason why I do what I do. And to my husband Joel, thank you for being the stability in my very busy life. Thank you for being my safe place. I love you!

And for you, dear reader, thank you for taking the time to read this book and allow these incredible authors to share their stories with you. May you step into being a conscious creator of your life and know you have the power to transform it.